i'm a good dog

i'm a good dog

Pit Bulls, America's Most Beautiful (and Misunderstood) Pet

KEN FOSTER

Viking Studio

VIKING STUDIO
Published by the Penguin Group
Penguin Group (USA) Inc., 375 Hudson Street,
New York, New York 10014, U.S.A.
Penguin Group (Canada), 90 Eglinton Avenue East, Suite 700,
Toronto, Ontario, Canada M4P 2Y3
(a division of Pearson Penguin Canada Inc.)
Penguin Books Ltd, 80 Strand, London WC2R 0RL, England
Penguin Ireland, 25 St. Stephen's Green, Dublin 2, Ireland
(a division of Penguin Books Ltd)
Penguin Books Australia Ltd, 250 Camberwell Road, Camberwell,
Victoria 3124, Australia
(a division of Pearson Australia Group Pty Ltd)
Penguin Books India Pvt Ltd, 11 Community Centre, Panchsheel Park,
New Delhi—110 017, India
Penguin Group (NZ), 67 Apollo Drive, Rosedale, Auckland 0632,
New Zealand (a division of Pearson New Zealand Ltd)
Penguin Books (South Africa) (Pty) Ltd, 24 Sturdee Avenue,
Rosebank, Johannesburg 2196, South Africa

Penguin Books Ltd, Registered Offices:
80 Strand, London WC2R 0RL, England

First published in 2012 by Viking Studio,
a member of Penguin Group (USA) Inc.

3 5 7 9 10 8 6 4 2

Copyright © becker&mayer!, Ltd., 2012
Text copyright © Ken Foster, 2012
All rights reserved

Published by arrangement with becker&mayer!, LLC, Bellevue, WA.
www.beckermayer.com

ISBN 978-0-670-02620-3

Printed in the United States of America
Set in Minister

Editor: Kristin Mehus-Roe
Designer: Katie Benezra
Photo researcher: Kara Stokes
Managing editor: Amelia Riedler
becker&mayer! pit bulls: Nelson, Milkdud, Patches, Rudy, and Pokey

PEARSON

In memory of Sula, and my parents.

CONTENTS

LEFT For close to 10 million Americans, it's a blocky-headed pit bull type that awaits them at home.

just dogs:
an introduction

BY THE TIME I LEARNED WHAT A PIT BULL REALLY was, it was too late; I was already in love. Of course I'd heard the stories, but I had never put these almost mythological urban tales together with the dogs in my neighborhood. I was living in Manhattan, just blocks away from a dog park, and dog watching was a spectator sport among those of us who were still dogless. There were dogs of every shape and size, but my eye kept going to the short, stocky, exuberant dogs that seemed like cartoons.

LEFT The mythology of pit bulls rarely matches the real thing.

You could tell by the gleam in their eye they felt very lucky to be here, in the city, walking with the person they kept on the other end of a leash. Their heads were blocky and human. Their short coats made it seem like they were wearing costumes made of felt. It wasn't hard to imagine there might be a little person inside. And they were everywhere that there were people: in cafés, outside bodegas, eating at restaurants.

By the time I'd decided to take the plunge into the world of dog ownership, I knew this was the dog for me. Nothing fancy, just an American dog. I was too shy to ask what kind of dog they might be—it seemed so personal!—but finally I broke down and popped the question. It was a girl dog named Dumpling, and the man walking her said, "She's a pit bull." Dumpling smiled at me and wagged her tail; this was not the image I had in mind when I heard the words *pit bull*. In fact, I didn't really have any particular image in mind—that's how little I'd concerned myself with the world of dogs.

So I immediately began searching for a pit bull I might adopt. I lived in a tiny one-room apartment, but I figured living with me and going for long walks through the day would be better than staying at a shelter. I went to the ASPCA's facility on the Upper East Side and fell in love with a sad black pit bull named Mauro, but he seemed too big for me. Then I found a dog named Baby on Petfinder and went to Brooklyn's BARC shelter to meet him. He was kind of skinny and lean and had a striped coat that was like nothing I'd ever seen, and his name had been changed from Baby to Brando. He didn't look anything like Dumpling, but I fell in love with him as soon as our eyes met. He seemed fragile and eager, and I began to worry about him as soon as I left the shelter. It didn't matter so much what his breed was. I fell in love with the individual quirks that made him who he was: his immediate bond with his people, his separation anxiety when his people were gone, his ability to convince me that we should nap together within the first five minutes we were home.

ACROSS Brando, the pit bull who isn't really a pit bull.

But even though he didn't look like any dog *I'd* seen before, other people thought he was a pit bull, too. His primary pit bull trait was that striped brindle coat, which people often mistake as breed-specific when in fact there is a wide variety of dogs who share it. The staff at the shelter decided to list him as a "shepherd mix" on his city license, so, they told me, no one would "come knocking on my door." It became clear to me, confusing as it was, that a single drop of pit bull blood in a dog's lineage designated it as a lower form of dog in the eyes of some, regarded with suspicion and stripped of its individual rights.

Yet it wasn't until years later that I really understood the predicament that pit bulls were in. By this time I was living in Florida, and I opened my door one day to find a small black-and-white pit bull waiting to greet me. She was compact and muscular, and it seemed that each part of her body was of equal proportion: head, torso, rump. She was a classic pit bull, and

LEFT Ken Foster with Sula on their New Orleans stoop.

when I called the local animal organizations, no one would help.

I brought her home, temporarily, I thought, and then we fell in love. And when you fall in love with a pit bull—and you inevitably will, if you meet one, fall in love—you need to be prepared to answer a lot of questions from skeptics on the street. "Why would you have a pit bull?" they ask, and sometimes they aren't quite that polite.

Does the fact that people question our pit bull love make it that much more intense? Possibly—because, in the case of Sula, I know that I saved her life, and despite what some people say, saving an animal's life is never a selfless act; there are huge emotional rewards. Like all forbidden love, from Romeo and Juliet on down the line, each time anyone questions or disapproves of our love, we defiantly love each other even more than before. But I think, like most other pit bull owners I know, that my love of Sula had more to do with this: She made me laugh; she had the good sense to turn and run away from bad music on the street; she liked to hug. And she loved to play practical jokes like hiding my glasses while I was taking a bath. We even had our own song: Corinne Bailey Rae's "Like a Star" was, I am certain, written for us.

Sula changed my life in a different way from Brando, because it was her idea, it seemed, to move on in. And I accepted her proposal, without having any idea how it would work out. She also changed me because there wasn't a day that people didn't judge her solely on how she looked.

Pit bulls are devoted. They are known to sing, proudly, in ridiculously operatic voices. I know pit bulls who have nursed kittens and another who adopted a piglet as its own. And this I know from photographs of them in New Orleans wading through water up to their necks: when you take away their unmistakable dog bodies, their round skulls and even-set eyes make them look remarkably like infants or old, bald men, or occasionally like the overly pancaked face of Judy Garland in decline. And like infants, old men, and Judy Garland, pit bulls are capable of expressing anguish and despair, as well as their euphoric joy in being alive.

13

What did I do before pit bulls? Sometimes I can't remember, no matter how hard I try. I went to the movies. I found the time to read every magazine to which I subscribed. I wrote books and magazine articles in which not a single animal appeared. I traveled incessantly. Yet I don't recall much joy in any of those things. Pit bulls expect more than just being a pet, so eventually, I rearranged my priorities to fit them in. Increasingly, they were the subjects of my work, and even when I was writing about people, it was the pit bulls of the world who took on the role of my muse.

Sula, who is no longer with me, lives on in the foundation I named after her. One of the things she taught me is that there is a whole world of people who love their pit bulls, and everyone else's too. The Sula Foundation is completely volunteer-run, and we work to educate and promote responsible pit bull ownership in New Orleans and beyond. We do some rescue, but most of what we do is build relationships with other pit bull owners, through low-cost vaccination clinics, spay/neuter programs, training, and advocacy. Through this work, I've become embedded in a social fabric that wraps above, beside, and below my own. Pit bulls are what we have in common, and once it is known

ACROSS Pit bulls can convey an incredible joy at being alive.

RIGHT The Sula Foundation was inspired by the author's first pit bull, Sula.

that we have that in common, all other social barriers are gone.

But there is still work to do. I have a T-shirt that reads "I Love My Pit Bull" in groovy 1970s-style lettering. Actually, I have three of these shirts, so that I know there is always one clean and ready to wear. (I also have shirts that read "my pit bull is a SAINT" and "Pit Bulls for

Peace"—all part of a series of shirts designed to raise funds for the Sula Foundation.) People see me wearing them and ask where I found them, or they point and say, "That's funny!" because they know pit bulls as dogs that are undeserving of anyone's love.

"But I do love my pit bull," I tell them, and then, if one of my dogs is with me, I might demonstrate the famously enthusiastic pit bull kiss.

That is what we do when we truly love things, whether dogs or people or works of art. We want to show them off in the best possible light.

So this is my introduction. Some people might say that my point of view is a little bit skewed. And to them I say that the answer should be clear on every page that follows. Yes. Absolutely, yes.

RIGHT Pit bulls are known and loved for their kisses.

what's in a pit bull?

WIGGLY. THAT'S THE WORD MOST OFTEN USED by pit bull owners to describe their dogs. Others are *loyal, compassionate, devoted, affectionate, couch potato, courageous, lapdog, snugglepuss, heroic, kissy-faced, lovebug, bed hog, pansy, soul mate, family.*

And if you let them, pit bull owners will never hesitate to tell you how they first met their doggy love. How they had never been a dog person before, but then they stumbled upon this dog: at a shelter, on the street, after reluctantly agreeing to look after a neighbor's dog before learning it was a pit bull. They will tell you that this dog, this pit bull, was so much different from what they'd been led to expect. This dog loved them.

Or they will tell you that their family has kept pit bulls for generations; this was the dog that waited every day for them to return from school. They may tell you they had never realized that there was another kind of dog, or that there were people who felt differently about pit bulls than they and everyone in their family did.

You might also talk to breeders, who speak about bloodlines—Boudreaux and Razor's Edge—and weight-pulling competitions, and you may realize, in spite of what some people say, that these people love their dogs, too. You might realize this while sitting on the sidewalk with the breeder's sixty-pound dog in your lap; or maybe it is the opposite, and you are the one who is trying to get the dog to climb on top of you to say hello, but it won't listen to you because it is just too well-behaved.

Pit bulls are smart. They are athletic. They can be trained to do just about anything, including leaping through the precise markers of an agility course, or competing in Frisbee and flyball.

In fact, the words pit bull owners use to describe their dogs aren't much different from the words other dog owners use to portray the dogs that have wormed their way into their hearts. The pit bull crowd may be a bit more passionate with their expressions of appreciation, but then so are their dogs. Pit bulls are known for their determination to give kisses. It's not unusual for a pit bull to drench the entire face and head of a human they haven't seen for a while—or even for just a few hours. They run to greet their masters, hips swiveling like Elvis, and perform happy dances on their arrival home. They love to love, and they love being loved, which is what makes it so easy to fall in love with them, too.

But what is a pit bull, anyway? *That* is the question that can turn the scene from collective cheerleading to something resembling a high school debate. Like a Rorschach inkblot, the pit bull means a number of different things—and different dogs—depending on an individual's point of view.

ACROSS A pit bull greets her owner after a few minutes of separation.

For some lovers of the American pit bull terrier (a breed recognized by the United Kennel Club (UKC), but not the American Kennel Club (AKC), although at one time, the same dog could be registered under the UKC as an American pit bull terrier and the AKC as an American Staffordshire terrier), *pit bull* is embraced as shorthand for their breed. However, fans of the American Staffordshire terrier and English Staffordshire terrier are usually quick to tell you that their breeds are not pit bulls.

To the general public, all three dogs are perceived as pit bulls, along with variations of the American bulldog, bull terriers, bullmastiffs, and even boxers, as well as mixes of these breeds.

The term "pit bull" is used to describe 10 to 20 percent of the dogs found in the United States, including pit bull–type breeds, indeterminate breeds, and breed mixes. These dogs may or may not be

---

LEFT & ACROSS Despite their differing looks and lineage, any of these dogs may signify "pit bull" to many people, from the large-headed Staffie type at the left to the bull terrier and more typical American pit bull terrier type at the right.

What's in a Pit Bull?

related to the American pit bull terrier, the American Staffordshire terrier, or the English Staffordshire terrier. But regardless of their true origins, in the eyes of most people—including the media and the law—these dogs are called pit bulls (or bullies or pit bull types).

In her 1991 book *Bandit: Dossier of a Dangerous Dog*, Vicki Hearne, a poet and dog trainer, addressed the overlapping shorthand that has been used to identify the dogs: "Note that . . . 'Bulldog' refers to a breed registered by the American Kennel Club, whereas 'bulldog' is either a type of breed or, more frequently, a nickname for the American Pit Bull Terrier. 'Bull Terrier' is an AKC breed . . . but bull terrier is a type of breed that includes Bull Terriers, American Staffordshire Terriers, Staffordshire Bull Terriers, American Pit Bull Terriers, and so on."

Testifying in a court case regarding the titular Bandit, Vicki Hearne said: "He may be an American Pit Bull Terrier, but is also possibly an Argentinian Dogo, a Swinford Bandog, an Olde Bulldogge, a Dogue

---

ACROSS For those who live with an endearing pit bull face, depictions of aggressive pit bulls do not match their experience.

de Bourdeaux, an American Bulldog, or an American Pit Bull Dog. (This latter breed is distinct from the American Pit Bull Terrier.)"

Even the legal definitions of the breed leave a lot of room for debate. In Denver, breed-specific legislation (BSL) banning pit bulls within the city limits offered this incredibly broad description: "A 'pit bull,' is defined as any dog that is an American Pit Bull Terrier, American Staffordshire Terrier, Staffordshire Bull Terrier, or any dog displaying the majority of physical traits of any one (1) or more of the above breeds, or any dog exhibiting those distinguishing characteristics which substantially conform to the standards established by the American Kennel Club or United Kennel Club for any of the above breeds" (*Dias v. City & County of Denver*, 567 F.3d 1169, 1173 [10th Cir. Colo. 2009]).

Essentially any dog that looked like what someone might think a pit bull looks like was banned from Denver.

WHAT IS A PIT BULL, ANYWAY?

Traditional pits (as opposed to the wide variety currently being bred, intentionally and accidentally) tend to be medium-sized, although they can vary from thirty to ninety pounds. They have an athletic, muscular body and a short coat, which makes their physical characteristics more apparent than those of furrier, longer-haired dogs. Their ears drop in loose triangles unless they've been cropped, and their intact tails are long and ratlike and always, always moving. Like most terriers, they have a strong prey drive for chasing rodents or cats or, preferably, toys.

As popular as the breed has been, its physical conformation—or traits—has a rather wide and vague definition. Even the UKC American pit bull terrier standard has a range of size, from thirty to sixty pounds. The majority of the dogs called "pit bulls" don't entirely meet the standards set forth for either the American pit bull terrier or the American Staffordshire terrier.

The UKC defines the American pit bull terrier less on its physical appearance than on its personality and ability to work: "a dog that combined the gameness of the terrier with the strength and athleticism of the Bulldog. The result was a dog that embodied all of the virtues attributed to great warriors: strength, indomitable courage, and gentleness with loved ones."

TRUE AMERICAN

Even if they don't know what a pit bull is, most people are familiar with its cousin, the English bull terrier. If you've seen a Target ad or remember Spuds MacKenzie, you know the ridiculous, egg-shaped head of this stalky comic dog. Like the rest of the bull and terrier mixes, the original ancestors of Spuds were created in the British Isles in the mid-1800s, less than a century after the American Revolution.

The generally accepted history of the group of dogs known as pit bulls is this: a cross between bulldogs and terriers, pit bull–type dogs originated in England, Ireland, and Scotland in the mid- to late 1800s. Bred for both their tenacity and their hearty physique, they were used as sporting dogs in a number of tasks, including bull baiting, hog hunting, and dogfighting. The "pit" of

ACROSS The UKC standard for the APBT describes the breed as gentle with loved ones.

the breed's name refers to the bull pit, where the dogs would help their masters corner large prey, like any other hunting dog might do.

These so-called bull and terriers were said to be dogs bred by crossing Old English bulldogs (now essentially extinct) and terriers. The breeding led

to two types of dogs: English bull terriers and Staffordshire bull terriers. Both looked quite similar in the 1800s (actually, quite like an American pit bull terrier, according to photographs from the time), but later diverged to become the bull terriers and the Staffordshire terriers we know today.

It's enough to make one's head spin. But, in fact, the easiest way to understand how *indistinct* the pit bull breeds may be is to create a diagram of all breeds that descend from the Old English bulldog, including the Staffordshire terrier, American Staffordshire terrier, American pit bull terrier, bull terrier, boxer, bullmastiff, English bulldog, American bulldog, and the French bulldog. They and their mixes share many of the same traits, though in varying degrees of proportion. All are mistaken for American pit bull terriers (and lumped—for all intents and purposes, as indicated by the Denver BSL—into the pit bull group). At the center of the diagram, you might want to reserve a spot for the dog sitting in front of you—pit bull or not—which is, in one way or another, related to the lot of them.

Stacey Coleman, executive director of the Animal Farm Foundation, a not-for-profit dedicated to securing equal opportunity for pit bull dogs, says, "I am yet to find two interpretations of histories of *pit bull* that agree!

ACROSS William Weekes's painting *The Visitor* depicts a family pit bull in the nineteenth century.

When we are asked about the history of pit bulls we talk about the general history of dogs, and since pit bulls are dogs, they go along for the ride. It gets sticky (and misleading) when we start talking about 'historically bred for' as if it tells us anything relevant about pit bulls today. If we use 'historically bred for' . . . for any kind of dogs, especially a group of dogs like those called pit bulls that have no agreed-upon pedigree or even phenotype, we are showing an unsophisticated understanding of dog breeding, dog genetics, and dog behavior. I cannot advise you on how to talk about the history of pit bulls without first finding a consensus on what a pit bull is. And if you can determine what a pit bull is, I am nominating you for the Nobel Prize!"

I am making no plans to head to Stockholm for the ceremony in the coming years.

In *Bandit*, Hearne wrote: "At the time of this writing, many Americans believe that there is a breed of dog that is irredeemably, magically vicious. . . . The dog in question is said to be good at guarding dope dens, to suffer from something called the Jekyll-Hyde syndrome, to be an indiscriminate killer of tires, weeds, kittens,

29

Vicki Hearne and Bandit

In the summer of 1986, the poet and dog trainer Vicki Hearne met Bandit, a "pit bull" who wasn't really a pit bull. Bandit was on death row at a Connecticut animal shelter for biting his owner. Bandit's owner had been beating him with a stick when he bit him, but the courts had determined that Bandit was a pit bull and that his behavior had been motivated by this idea of what he was.

Hearne had never intended to keep Bandit. She had simply asked the court to allow her to train the dog; if he passed the American Temperament Test, they would allow him to live. (Of course, pit bulls have historically scored very well on the ATT, outscoring more-popular breeds like the golden retriever, but no one involved in this case had the benefit of such information.) Hearne's goal was to save Bandit and return him to his owner, who she felt had been as misjudged as Bandit himself.

Bandit became a poster child for pit bulls at the time. Hearne wrote a book about him (*Bandit: Dossier of a Dangerous Dog*), and the pair were featured in the Oscar-nominated short documentary *A Little Vicious*. Novelist Katharine Weber remembers that Hearne would often bring Bandit over to swim with Weber's children in the family pond. "Bandit was a big wuss," Weber says. "The kids loved him, and he was really just a clown." Bandit even made the cover of *Smithsonian* magazine.

Hearne was an eccentric, to be sure, and as the case against Bandit dragged on in the courts, she began to blur the lines between her creative efforts and her work on behalf of the dog. In an effort to raise funds and solicit support among her literary friends, Hearne began sending out newsletters reporting on Bandit's progress and the absurd logic of many of the officials against whom she was expected to defend him (and, by extension, all pit bull–type dogs). Printed at home on her dot matrix printer, the newsletter took on the name *The American "Pit Bull" Defense Association*, to which she eventually added *and Literary Society*.

In the documentary *A Little Vicious*, Hearne is shown chain-smoking as she rambles on about the expectations humans placed on Bandit and other dogs and the dogs' desire to work. But the highlight of the film shows Bandit as he passes poker-faced through each phase of his tempera-ment test—including people jumping out from behind bushes and throwing umbrellas open in his face. The expression on

ACROSS Vicki Hearne and Bandit are shown together.

Bandit's face seems to mirror what the audience is thinking: *these people are crazy!*

After passing the ATT, the court would allow Bandit to survive only under two conditions: He could never enter the Stamford city limits, and he had to live the rest of his life with Vicki Hearne. "It's true that pit bulls grab and hold on," she wrote. "But what they most often grab and refuse to let go of is your heart, not your arm."

and people, to exert two thousand or sometimes twenty thousand pounds of pressure per square inch with its double- or triple-jointed jaws. . . . These dogs are popularly called 'pit bulls.' They don't exist."

The mythical idea of the monster pit bull had taken such a strong hold that the term no longer applied to the actual pit bull dogs—or any other dog that actually lived.

THE CASE OF DNA

A few years ago, when it was still rare to see a pit bull's image featured in the media (and certainly not in a purely joyful, positive way), my eye was caught by an art review in the weekend section of the local paper. Featured among the paintings of artist Sandy Chism, there was a portrait of a smiling, happy pit bull, a part of her exhibition titled Small Wonders. The show was opening that night, and although I'd never purchased a painting before, I knew that this painting had to be mine. I raced to the gallery to put my name on it. At the gallery, my perspective was thrown off by the appearance of the actual painting. It was large, as big, at least, as an actual pit bull. But in person it was clear that the model wasn't a real dog at all; it was a painting of a shiny porcelain pit bull figurine, enlarged to the size of a real dog. The painting was an illusion, playing on our expectations of the image of a pit bull. The painting's title was *It's in My Nature*.

It's in their nature. This is a phrase pit bull owners hear all too often. For better or worse, the adage goes, our dog's behavior is attributed to their DNA. A dog's behavior, people say, is predicted by its breeding, making it inevitably a great family dog, a great hunter, or an alert guard dog. But most of these people are just repeating notions that have been handed down like folklore, rather than via the study of genetics.

It is a notion of predicting behavior that we would never claim in humans. (Or maybe we would: The French are snobs; the Irish are hot-tempered; Germans are rigid. And according to my muttlike heritage, I must be all three.) But with the advent of DNA testing, researchers have been able to, for the first time, look

———————————————

ACROSS The painting *It's in My Nature* by Sandy Chism plays on our expectations.

beyond the mere appearance of a dog to find out their genetic origins. And what they've found is that, in the case of dogs identified as pit bulls, there is virtually no indication that they are anything other than a particular family of mixed breeds.

Some of the breeds that show up include, of course, bull terriers and bulldogs, but also golden retrievers, cocker spaniels, Labradors, Bernese mountain dogs, a variety of hounds, boxers, Dalmatians, and various other terriers.

A few years ago, a beauty queen named Bernann McKinney was so bonded with her adopted pit bull, Booger, she negotiated for a $150,000 cloning procedure when he was diagnosed with cancer. The result: five dogs that had an exact DNA match with the original dog (confirmed with additional DNA testing)—yet they didn't look or, more important, *act* like the original at all.

ACROSS A pit bull's genetic background appears to have little effect on its personality.

RIGHT Pit bull owners, however, claim their dogs sleep even more than other dogs.

35

Diane Jessup: The Maverick

We all love pit bulls in different ways, sometimes with such difference that the only thing we agree on is that we do love them. One particular area of disagreement is breeding. Many rescuers feel that the overpopulation of the breed needs to be addressed by a ban on breeding; others feel that only responsible breeding will preserve the qualities we love most.

And then there is Diane Jessup, an American pit bull trainer who has been a pit bull advocate since long before it became a trending topic on Twitter. Her work with the dogs has included training them for service with the Washington State Police.

"The single biggest challenge facing our breed is the unfortunate belief that breeding is somehow bad," says Jessup. "You have people out there who say they are 'pro-pit bull' with bumper stickers that say things like 'Save a Pit Bull—Kill a Breeder.'

"An ethical breeder puts the stewardship of the breed ahead of their own gain or goals," she says. "*They do not produce animals for the simple purpose of resale*. I like to think that a responsible breeder produces outstanding examples of the breed and also owns a rescue or two. . . . very, very few people should breed—but everyone who loves the breed should be a patron of a breeder they respect."

ABOVE Many pit bulls have been trained to work with law enforcement programs. Pictured here is a U.S. Customs dog with his handler.

The DNA was not a predictor of the dogs' individual behaviors. (McKinney was so disappointed that she threatened to sue the Korean company that had manufactured her new set of dogs.)

More recently, Janis Bradley, an author and dog trainer at the Dog Training Internship Academy, researched the whole question of dog breed as a predictor of behavior and found that an individual dog's behavior had surprisingly little to do with its heritage, even in breeds that are still traditionally bred for particular skills (such as greyhounds). On the subject of the pit bull heritage, she told me this:

"To call a dog a *pit bull* is completely meaningless for at least three reasons. What people generally mean by this is a group of dogs, related in some way or another, who are genetically predetermined to be hyperaggressive, often toward both other dogs and humans. If such a group existed, it would certainly be useful to know about it. This imagined group does not exist.

<hr />

RIGHT A dog labeled a "pit bull" may look or act quite differently than another dog with the same label.

"First, the majority are labeled this way because of some aspect of their appearance like head shape, and are, in fact, mixed breeds. You simply cannot identify breed composition in a mixed-breed dog this way, any more than you can pinpoint the ancestry of a person by hair color. A blocky-headed or muscular dog is as likely to be a descendant of Labrador retrievers or cocker spaniels as of American Staffordshire terriers.

"Second, many people believe there is a type of dog called 'pit bull' that encompasses various breeds, similar to herding dogs or sporting dogs. There has never been such a breed category, and even if there had been, we now have conclusive evidence that these kinds of functional 'types' no longer predict behavior in modern dog breeds.

"Finally, temperament studies of American Staffordshire terriers—the only actual breed generally acknowledged to have been consistently used back in the mists of time for dogfighting—have shown them (along with various other breeds sometimes categorized as pit bulls) to be no more aggressive today toward dogs or people than golden retrievers. So the term 'pit bull'

is one that, every time it is used, does the damage of making us think we have said something meaningful and action-worthy, when in fact we have said nothing at all."

Like any other term that we humans assign, the names we call the variations of the dogs in our midst may say more about us than we realize. Is a pit bull a measurable entity, or is it a set of ideas we express? Is it the big boxy head or the clownish spirit? Is the title *pit bull* something we impose on the dogs, or is it an honor they receive?

Sometimes, it is easier to define an object by the qualities it lacks. So I give you a list of things that are not true of a pit bull:

• Pit bulls do not attack like sharks. Or do anything like sharks do.

• Pit bulls do not have locking jaws, double jaws, or the ability to exert any more pressure than any other type of dog.

• Pit bulls' brains are not too large for their skulls.

———————————————————————

ACROSS Pit bulls are the subject of many myths. In reality, they are just dogs.

• Pit bulls were not bred for any one specific purpose.

So what is a pit bull? A pit bull is exuberant, affectionate, loyal, block-headed, athletic, ridiculous, occasionally stubborn, challenging, rewarding, and loved. A pit bull is American, and like most Americans these dogs are a jumble of DNA and contradictions, which is, naturally, what pit bull lovers love most about their dogs.

RIGHT Pit bulls are like all Americans, human or canine. Each is unique.

A Mix of Snugglepuss, Rubber, and Springs

The wonderful thing about Tiggers is Tiggers are wonderful things. Their tops are made out of rubber, their bottoms are made out of springs. . . .

When I watch my dogs playing, or when they are morphing their shapes next to me in bed like living memory foam, it is easy to think that Tigger, the bouncy, flouncy clown of a tiger in Winnie-the-Pooh, was really a misidentified brindle pit bull.

When I adopted my oldest dog, Brando, I didn't know much about owning a dog in the city, and even less about the idea that a particular breed could be swept up and euthanized based entirely on their appearance, or the breed mix listed on their licensing. Brando was brindle and he was supposedly close to full grown at thirty-five pounds. The volunteer who had scoured the Internet to find a non–pit bull match suggested he was a Belgian shepherd. Someone else thought he was a Plott hound. It was all a guess. This was before canine DNA tests were available, and I was really concerned with what breed he might be.

But then he kept growing. And growing. And growing. Is he a pit bull/whippet? we wondered in the dog park. Is he a pit bull/greyhound? Is he a pit bull/Great Dane? Eventually he peaked at a long-legged, long-torsoed 110 pounds. Even Brando seemed confused about what kind of dog he might be. He tried to romance two mastiff sisters but was too shy. He tried to join a pack of Rhodesian ridgebacks but couldn't keep up. His ridiculous snout had inspired me to ask him one morning if he might be a platypus. Still, I continued to call him a pit bull/Great Dane, because it was the easiest way of describing him to people he hadn't yet met.

Eight years later, canine DNA testing became the rage. The Sula Foundation had arranged to do a "Who's Your Daddy?" fund-raiser, and I decided to try it out on my own dogs as a test of whether they made any sense at all. I took a cheek-swab from Brando, and I took a swab from my Zephyr. And then I waited for the results to come back, as if this tiny bit of knowledge would help me in some way or tell me something I didn't know about the dogs who had been sharing my home for years.

Zephyr's results came back as a mix of Rottweiler and shepherd. Brando apparently came from a long line of mutts, with a distant trace of bullmastiff and hound dog. So much for his being a pit bull.

More recently, I sent in another DNA sample, this time from Douglas, a blue brindle pit bullish–looking dog who also likes to howl like a hound dog to warn people off our property. The first time he unleashed his banshee wail, I thought, *That's not a pit bull*. I suspected he might be a bulldog-Catahoula mix, though I didn't even know if such a thing might exist. So, in went the swab to the lab, and back came the results: bulldog and Bernese mountain dog.

The inside of a dog, generally speaking, has nothing to do with the outside of a dog, their behavior, or their appearance—and vice versa. We nod in agreement when a dog acts as we expect it to, and share our surprise when a Labrador refuses to swim. In the end, the only thing that my DNA experiment taught me was that my dogs are all ridiculously unique and idiosyncratic—and that's why, in my house, they all fit right in.

ACROSS Sometimes pit bulls seem to be made of rubber.

2

and a pit bull
makes three

LEFT Unaffected by the chaos of children, many pit bulls make excellent family dogs.

I FIRST MET CLEETUS AND HIS FAMILY ONE afternoon shortly after Hurricane Katrina, when I heard his unmistakable voice coming through my New Orleans neighborhood. There were so few people back that any voice—any sound—was startling. And this sounded like an old woman singing opera—although perhaps while also suffering from delusions or drunkenness. I ran out of my house to see what was going on and noticed other neighbors scattered along the streets standing at their

doors to see what was happening, too. There he was: a black-and-white pit bull singing at the top of his lungs as he strolled down the street with his family—a woman, child, and a toddler in a stroller. It was a grim time, but this dog was clearly very happy to be back in the neighborhood, and seeing him made me happy, too.

I was so struck by him that I immediately posted on our neighborhood's online forum: Does anyone know to whom the singing pit bull belongs?

Cleetus has pretty much the coolest family around. His dad, Chet, runs a crazy secondhand store; his mom, Laura, works at the zoo—and all three of them agree that it is the human kids in the family that always come first. One gets the sense that Cleetus could tell a really good story about their years together; he's been there from the beginning. But he's not talking, in spite of his capacity for singing.

Laura explains, "I was present for Cleetus's birth in

LEFT Cleetus is the center of his family.

ACROSS Whether a pit bull joins a family as a puppy or an adult, it is sure to become a treasured family member.

October of 1999." Cleetus was one of nine puppies born to Chessie, a black-and-white female owned by Laura's then boyfriend, Ron. Ron was a street kid and a railroad hopper, the kind of guy who might have been called a hobo a few decades back. And Laura was feeling newly free from her life in suburban Philadelphia.

And a Pit Bull Makes Three

"Watching Chessie give birth and eat the placentas of nine puppies was miraculous to me," she says, "as was watching her care for these helpless, always hungry pups."

Cleetus was the runt of the litter, and as they began to give the pups out to their friends, Laura realized this little dog, the tiniest and weakest of them, was really hers to take care of. Things with Laura and Cleetus went swimmingly; they spent long hours under the banana trees in the yard, working together on training. Ron wasn't as interested in stability, and soon Laura and Cleetus were on their own—which is when Chet showed up. The three of them were all coming off broken relationships—Chet's ex had run off with their one-year-old daughter—so somehow these three individuals fit together: man, woman, and dog.

Laura began teaching special education for a neighboring school district; Chet raised Cleetus as if he were his own, cuddling him, sketching pictures of him, taking him to get neutered while Laura worked.

ACROSS A pit bull can be the ultimate childhood companion.

When Chet and Laura started their own family, Cleetus took it in stride. Having a new baby meant he got less attention, but he never seemed to mind. "He seemed to instinctively know that Gavin was the new baby, and he needed to protect him," says Laura. Eventually another baby, Anya, followed; and then Chet's first daughter, Sescha, was reunited with them, making a family of five—or six, if you include Cleetus, which they always do.

They left New Orleans after Gavin developed lead poisoning from the city's famously contaminated soil, but moved back just in time to evacuate for Hurricane Katrina and then come back home again. Amid the chaos, it may have been Cleetus who managed to keep everyone together.

"Unlike me," Laura confides, "Cleetus adapted well to all this change. He was a great dog on the road, and a great family dog. He never minded putting his needs last. He was always content and happy. He joined me as I took the kids in a stroller on daily runs through our devastated neighborhood. He provided companionship and protection to all of us.

Milton

When Theo Cooper met his future wife, Allison, his winning the affection of her children was just one of the hurdles they faced. The other was whether their dogs would accept each other as family, as well. Allison's adopted pit mix, Rosie, was nine and set in her ways. Milton was just a puppy, still learning how to be a dog. They were both used to being the center of attention, so no one was sure how it might go.

"They were instant family," Theo says. "Rosie taught Milton everything, and he made her playful and puppylike."

But it is the unfolding relationship between Milton and the children, and their shared relationships with one another, that makes Theo proud of them all.

"It's an understanding relationship between our dogs and us," Matilda, age ten, explains; and her older sister, Dixie, age twelve, agrees.

Dixie says, "I couldn't live without a dog in my life, because I like having someone there when I'm lonely or scared. They're always there for you and we're always there for them. I used to be more shy when people asked about Milton, but now I'm more confident and I like to show him off and talk about him. Having pit bulls and learning more about them from watching shows like *Pit Boss* and *Pit Bulls and Parolees* has made me want to start volunteering at an animal shelter."

This gets Matilda thinking: "Why do all the pit bull shows have to have, like, something else? Like little people or guys who used to be in jail? Why can't there just be pit bull shows?"

Milton and Dixie even worked together on a class project, presenting her report on the misperception of pit bulls: ". . . my dad brought Milton in and he did some tricks in front of the class (Milton, not my dad). They were especially impressed when I threw meat treats on the ground and told him, 'Leave it!'—and he didn't touch it until I told him, 'Okay.'

"Milton taught me that it doesn't matter what other people think of you," Dixie says. "And he taught me to be more friendly. And the love of peanut butter."

More recently, the family shared one of the more bittersweet lessons that family dogs always teach us. Rosie became sick and passed away, and everyone, including Milton, went through a period of grieving. But things get easier with time, and with the support that only a family can bring. The girls think it's time to get Milton another pit bull to keep him company.

"Dad," Dixie asks, "when are we getting another one?"

ACROSS Milton is his girls' best friend.

"Until you asked me what Cleetus has meant to me and my family, I had never thought much about this," says Laura. "I felt, but did not think. But I know I love him as a family member, a friend, a protector."

DOGS IN THE FAMILY

Pit bulls seem particularly suited for life with kids. Brando's best friend in my Manhattan neighborhood was a full pit bull named Lugo, who was picky about who he was friends with. Lugo had been fished out of the East River, and he had inspired a short story by Dave Eggers. He didn't have time for just anyone. The first time they met, Brando walked over and climbed onto his back, with his legs dangling on either side of him. He wasn't going to give Lugo a choice in the matter. This became their game, climbing up and around each other, holding their positions very still for long moments of meditation before switching it up again. Watching their series of careful formations, his owner, Brent, suggested that they were trying to spell

---

ACROSS In general, pit bulls dislike baths as much as any dog.

something out with their bodies. I often wondered if Brando was trying to worm his way into a more interesting home than my own.

But then the baby arrived. Lugo loved his parents' baby; like most dogs, he immediately sensed the relationship between him, his people, and this new little body wrapped in blankets and onesies. Lugo took on a new sense of responsibility, and this bored Brando, the mutt, who tried to distract everyone by stealing the socks of the sleeping baby.

Jennifer Shryock knows the value a pit bull can bring to the home. "We have four dogs, and of the four Windsor is the best with the toddler," she says of her pit bull, Windsor. "His worst danger is his tail. We call him Mr. Enthusiastic; he will do anything to get their attention!" Shryock, along with her husband and three young children, has fostered more than seventy dogs in the past ten years. And don't even ask how many cats.

Windsor spent his first five years tethered in a yard twenty-four hours a day. Shryock's daughter Kayleigh was seven when she saw a photo of Windsor, starving at the end of a chain. People who view the

54

photographs today have a hard time recognizing the cheerful family dog.

It was just one of a hundred e-mails in her mother's in-box that day, asking for help with an abused dog. Kayleigh just happened to be there when her mother opened the photo and Windsor's sad face popped up. He looked skinny and confused. "Mommy," she said, "we need to help that dog." Now Windsor sleeps in Kayleigh's bed every night. Kayleigh worked with Windsor on his training and even created her own training demo for the family's foster dog blog. When you train a new dog, Shryock says, you learn right along with them—and so it was with Windsor as he adapted to life off a chain, and his family learned through his determination to win their hearts.

Shryock is the founder of Family Paws, an organization that aims to bring dogs and children together in healthy, safe relationships. Shryock's own childhood dog was a trusted confidant. "That was my sanity," she says, "to have an outlet to channel my creativity and just be with her. The life cycle is a huge lesson, not the happiest, but an important one. You're learning empathy and patience, unconditional acceptance. Letting my children develop their own individual relationships with our animals, under my guidance and supervision, has been an important lesson for me, as well."

The pit bull has been a family dog for more than a century—in other words, for as long as the dogs have

been known to exist, and the largest known collection of pit bull family photos is stored at Animal Farm Foundation. I flew up to Bangall, New York, to check it out, touching down at JFK, where I was only a few feet off the plane when someone spotted the pit bull on my T-shirt and immediately began talking as if we were old friends.

"Great dogs," he said, and I noticed that he was wearing a pit bull shirt, too, featuring Wallace, the former Frisbee champion. "You know," he said, "there's a great organization called Animal Farm Foundation; that's where I got my dogs." And then the photos came out. Big Al, a retired cop, loves to talk about his dogs and his grandchildren, and how well they all get along.

"I'm actually headed up there now," I confessed, and he made me promise to tell everyone hello when I got there.

The foundation operates on an enormous and beautiful working farm, which we toured on my arrival—the training facility, the horse barn, the dressage field, the rescued cow hiding behind a tree, the disc field, and finally, the museum, where glass

---

ACROSS It was Kayleigh Shryock who prompted her mother to rescue Windsor. The two are now the best of friends.

Albert

cases display hundreds of old photographs and tintypes (the precursor to paper photos), all featuring families and their pit bulls. In some, the children—dressed in their Sunday clothes—pose with the dog at their feet. In others, the entire family has gathered around, perhaps with a few visiting relatives. At the center of them all is the family pit bull. One particular pair of photos shows the two "Alberts." In the first, Albert is a small boy with his dog; in the second, Albert has grown up and married, and he is surrounded by his own wife and children . . . and their pit bull.

One of the earliest known newspaper accounts to use the term "pit bull" to describe a mixed breed was about a Milwaukee dog named Dixie, who was chosen as the city's most popular dog at the annual dog show in 1926. "The pit bull, pet of little 1-year-old Catherine Wright . . . will not compete with other dogs for honors," the *Milwaukee Sentinel* reported. "She is not pedigreed, not eligible to any except the miscellaneous class, but there she will reign supreme." Nowhere in the account does the reporter pause to editorialize on the significance of a pit bull being the city's most popular dog, or being the pet of a one year old. We can assume this is because there was nothing unusual about it at the time.

But when it comes to the pit bull as the ultimate childhood companion, fingers inevitably point to Petey and *The Little Rascals*. In dozens of short comedy films spanning the silent and early talking pictures, a medium-sized brindle-and-white pit bull, Petey, was the moral center of the *Our Gang* world (although his character did consider suicide to get his owner's attention in his first film, *Dog Heaven*). In other notable films, Petey was wrongly accused of stealing chickens in *Dogs Is Dogs*, and in *Pups Is Pups*, a litter of runaway pit bulls are lured to any ringing bell they hear, expecting supper. Finally, it is a church bell that reunites them with their owner.

Like our own (sometimes idealized) childhood dogs, Petey always kept an eye on the kids, offered an ear to listen and a shoulder to lean on, and he seemed to rise

---

ACROSS Albert is seen as a young boy with his pet pit bull.

RIGHT In this photo, the adult Albert is seen with his wife, children, and another pit bull.

Josh and Cass and Kady and Felix

HOW JOSH MET CASS:

My sister felt like I needed a dog because I'd been the victim of a violent crime. I knew I wanted Cass because of how crazy and loud he was when we got there to see the puppies! Later, I found out his crazy, erratic behavior was directly linked to the ceiling fan. He was and is mellow to this day, but turn on a ceiling fan and the dog goes nuts!

HOW KADY MET FELIX:

My high school student sent me text-message pictures of the puppies right after they were born, and I picked Felix immediately; he was the cutest. Felix was also the name of the student who gave him to me. I got him when he was only five and a half weeks old.

HOW JOSH AND CASS MET KADY AND FELIX:

So I'm at the dog park and up walks this girl who is obviously out of my league. She was dragging a white-and-brown hamster-looking dog called Felix. We'd never seen her there before, and I noticed she was also carrying "poop" bags. Well, at this park we didn't pick up poop! I blurted out, "We don't pick up shit here." She went on a rant about how she did. So I waited until lil' Felix pooped and as soon as she picked up this massive mess her dog created, I asked her where she was going to put it. Mind you, there were no trash cans. So there she stood with a bag of poop. Round one was mine!

HOW KADY AND FELIX MET JOSH AND CASS:

Josh realized very early on that I was in over my head when it came to Felix. He may have looked like a hamster, but he is and was a handful. It took a couple of months of casual interactions at the dog park before he asked me out. We went to a pet festival very early on; Cass was perfect and Felix misbehaved and pooped in the most awkward places. Josh started potty-training Felix while I was at work. He went by my apartment to let him out throughout the day. It was the most thoughtful thing anyone had ever done for me. As we got to know each other better, I realized what an amazing person Josh was in many, many ways. However, his passion for animals was what made me see it so quickly. Felix and I are so much better off now that he is in our lives.

Josh and Kady married in 2011; they share their bed with two pit bulls, a cat, and a parrot.

ACROSS Kady and Josh pose with their two dogs, Felix (L) and Cass (R).

above the chaos with a center of clarity that only a dog can possess. Like most stars of the silent era, the story of the dog actor who played Petey is the stuff of rumor and legend. Petey was first played by Pal the Wonder Dog, but his career and life were cut short when he was fed poison (or by some accounts, crushed glass). His replacement was his son, known as Lucenay's Peter, a registered American pit bull. Petey was so well trained that he even starred in his own short instructional film with his owner, Harry Lucenay, possibly the first dog-training "video" ever produced. When the cast arrived at Saint Joseph's orphanage in St. Louis for a visit in 1928, it was Petey who walked on two legs delivering boxes of candy tucked carefully in his mouth. Petey even made appearances on Atlantic City's Steel Pier, where children (including my uncles Pete and Jack) waited in line to have their photos taken with Petey nuzzling their necks, or posing above them with a pipe tucked firmly between his lips.

ACROSS In 1928, Petey and his gang bring candy to children at Saint Joseph's orphanage.

Actor Jackie Cooper remembered Petey decades later in his memoir, recalling a weekend he was allowed to take Petey home for a sleepover. "To stay a whole weekend with Pete was my idea of glory and paradise combined."

Harry Lucenay's son remembers Petey fondly, saying, "He was gentle, playful and warm. He would sleep at the foot of my bed. He was just the regular family dog. I really miss him."

AN ELEPHANT'S FAITHFUL, ONE HUNDRED PERCENT!

Perhaps Theodor Seuss Geisel, also known as Dr. Seuss, was thinking about a pit bull when he wrote about a pachyderm's loyalty.

When Geisel was growing up in Springfield, Massachusetts, he had an ally in his dog, Rex. Rex was a pit bull with a limp—he had all four of his legs but walked on only three—and wherever the two went, the other boys in town made fun of them. It was 1914, and anti-German sentiment was strong, so Theodor must have found some comfort in having Rex

as a friend, sharing their outsider status. When Ted began drawing, Rex was his first subject, though in his imagination he began with revising Rex's form into that of a horse, rather than a dog.

It is easy to see how the influence of Rex may have inspired Seuss's moral sensibility. In *Horton Hears a Who*, the faithful elephant teaches everyone that "a person's a person, no matter how small." In the *Grinch Who Stole Christmas*, it is the Grinch's dog, Max, who demonstrates loyalty to a master, even if his heart is two sizes too small.

ABOVE Dr. Seuss's whimsical style and moral sensibility may have had an early influence from his pit bull, Rex.

ACROSS Many pit bulls share Rex Thurber's love of swimming.

In the world of Dr. Seuss, respecting individuality was always primary to being a whole person—or a whole Who.

DOG WISH

Rex must have been a popular name among pit bull–owning children who were destined to become cartoonists and humorists. Like Seuss, James Thurber loved dogs. In particular, he loved a dog also named Rex, a childhood pet. "'An American Bull Terrier', we used to say, proudly; none of your English bulls," Thurber wrote. Thurber admitted to dreaming of Rex for decades after his death.

And a Pit Bull Makes Three

Thurber was unique in many ways, perhaps most particularly in his love of dogs, which included an appreciation for even their less-attractive, most doglike behavior. In his essay "Snapshot of a Dog," he describes all the noble attributes of his childhood companion. "I shall always remember that shining, virgin dive," Thurber writes of the day Rex discovered a love of swimming after leaping spontaneously from the banks of the river. "Then he swam upstream and back just for the pleasure of it, like a man. It was fun to see him battle upstream against a stiff current, struggling and growling every foot of the way."

In another escapade, Rex spent the night retrieving a chest of drawers, determined to bring it back to the family home—for reasons no one could quite discern. "There were no drawers in the chest when he got it home, and it wasn't a good one—he hadn't taken it out of anybody's house; just an old cheap piece that somebody had abandoned on a trash heap," wrote Thurber. "Still, it was something he wanted, probably because it presented a nice problem in transportation. It tested his mettle. We first knew about his achievement

when, deep in the night, we heard him trying to get the chest up onto the porch. It sounded as if two or three people were trying to tear the house down. We came downstairs and turned on the porch light. Rex was on the top step trying to pull the thing up, but it had caught somehow and he was just holding his own. I suppose he would have held his own until dawn if we hadn't helped him. The next day we carted the chest miles away and threw it out. If we had thrown it out in a nearby alley, he would have brought it home again, as a small token of his integrity in such matters."

Rex lived a full life, but he didn't last long enough— that's the problem with most dogs we love. And for Thurber, all it took was unexpectedly coming across his photo, twenty-five years later, to vividly recall their love.

THE DEFENDER

Ledy VanKavage is senior legislative attorney for Best Friends Animal Society, a sanctuary in Utah that also

---

ACROSS Ledy VanKavage's lifetime of animal advocacy began with a pit bull named Boody.

works on behalf of animals throughout the country. Her work takes her nationwide, where she addresses laws that unfairly target family dogs due to their apparent breeds.

She was four years old when her mother took her to visit her Lithuanian grandmother on the other side of town. There she met a small stray pit bull that her grandmother was planning to give to Ledy's aunt. But "it was love at first sight," Ledy says. She named him Boody. "He went everywhere with me."

"We lived out in the country in Collinsville, Illinois," she says. "It was the height of irresponsible dog

And a Pit Bull Makes Three

ownership." Dogs were allowed to roam, and no one thought of having a male dog neutered.

"I thought he was a Boston terrier, because . . . that was the closest match I could find. He was my best friend. When I was in trouble I'd go hide with him in the doghouse."

One day, outside the grocery store, Boody joined in a scuffle between two other dogs. Little Ledy grabbed him by his collar and led him away to hide behind a tree. "I was terrified that the police would shoot him," she says. Later, when the coast was clear, she and Boody headed home under the safe escort of her young friends.

When Boody passed away at six, the family moved on to German shepherds, which were then regarded as the dog we all should fear. "I remember walking my shepherd down the street as a girl. A woman stopped me and said, 'That dog is going to eat your face.'"

It wasn't until law school that Ledy realized for the first time that Boody, her childhood friend, was now considered to be "dangerous." By then, she and her husband had a Lab mix named Trotsky. When they went to the shelter to find him a companion, they found a brindle puppy that they were told was a Great Dane. Ledy knew immediately that he was actually a pit bull, labeled as a Great Dane so that he could be placed for adoption. The shelter wasn't officially allowed to adopt out pit bulls.

ACROSS Karma is the newest pit bull to join Ledy's brood.

"My husband was worried that he would be too big for our house," remembers Ledy. "So I had to explain that he wasn't really going to get that much bigger." They named him Darwin. "Survival of the fittest," Ledy says. It was her love for Darwin the pit bull that inspired her to put her legal skills to work defending dogs. When a neighboring town proposed breed-discriminatory legislation in 1987, she fought it and won. ("Politics is not a spectator sport," she likes to remind people.)

Darwin was followed by Clarence Darrow, Jane Goodall, Che Guevara, and Bella Abzug—all pit bull–type dogs rescued from area shelters. Their newest addition is Karma, one of hundreds of dogs seized in a Missouri dogfighting case. While Ledy fights breed discrimination across the country, she and her husband remain species neutral at home; in addition to the pit bulls, they also maintain a feral cat colony. "Karma," she says, "loves to take care of the kittens."

FAMILY RESEMBLANCE

When people talk about their families, they invariably turn to family resemblances: who looks like whom,

who acts like one side of the family or the other. While I don't claim that my dogs are my children—or worse, my fur babies—I admit that there are times when I see characteristics in them that I attribute to some sort of family trait, almost like sharing DNA. In these moments, Brando is the spitting image of my paternal grandfather, Russell Foster, a banker who had a very serious analytic temperament but arranged his lunch break so that he could run home to watch *All My Children* with his wife. (In fact, for years when I left Brando at home in the afternoon, I left the television set on so that he could catch the soaps, as well.) At other times, he also evokes my brother, Christopher, the actor, for his love of performance and his occasional emotional outbursts. Zephyr has my mother's eyes and my sister's sense of practicality; she can make any situation work. And Sula, while she was with me, was

ACROSS Pit bulls need families as much as we need them in our families.

RIGHT A boy and his dog. Pit bull mix Nelson was adopted through PAWS near Seattle, Washington.

69

the exact mirror of myself: stubborn, anxiety prone, resistant to any change.

In this way, my dogs are my family. And like all family members, our pit bulls help shape us. I feel certain that Cleetus, sly as he was, had a definite hand (or paw) in assembling a family around himself, just as my own dogs have conspired to move me into larger houses, with larger yards and more room for them to adopt companions for themselves. (Yes, I credit Brando with the decision making regarding subsequent dogs in the house; once a dog has acquired his approval, I am powerless to dissuade him.) Just as Kayleigh spotted Windsor on her mother's computer and knew that he was hers to help. And just as Darwin the pit bull inspired Ledy in her work. They may not be fur babies, but they are dogs. And they are family.

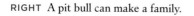

RIGHT A pit bull can make a family.

the comeback

I MET DAISY AND ANNIE ON A BEAUTIFUL, SUNNY
day in Oklahoma, at a small animal shelter somewhere
outside Tulsa. Daisy and Annie didn't have names yet; they
were simply kennel number three and kennel number four,
two of a dozen dogs that were there in hiding, waiting for
evaluation before being transferred to pit bull rescue
organizations, or being euthanized if it came to that.

I had flown in on short notice to meet Tim Racer
from BAD RAP, an Oakland, California, advocacy group
that had been called in as consultants. I didn't have any
particular expertise in evaluating fighting dogs, but I was

LEFT After being considered
pariahs for almost twenty years,
pit bulls are beginning to regain
their status.

hoping to gain some. We'd all underestimated the difficulty of getting from New Orleans to Oklahoma, but at a certain point there was no turning back.

On July 8, 2009, more than 350 dogs were seized in a raid on an eight-state dogfighting ring. The majority of the dogs were kenneled in a warehouse in St. Louis while the case dragged out. In dogfighting cases, the dogs are often held for months or even years as evidence for the potential court proceedings that will follow. In this case, there were several pockets of dogs whose owners relinquished them, making it possible for animal rescue organizations to step in and evaluate them for adoption before the restless behaviors associated with longtime kenneling set in.

These were the remnants of the dark days for pit bulls. In spite of their century of goodwill toward men, women, and children, the public perception of America's best dog had taken a turn. Pit bull–type dogs have always been used for the puzzling sport of animal fighting, as have Boston terriers, Jack Russells, bulldogs, mastiffs, and roosters. But beginning in the 1980s, the tough image associated with dogfighting also inspired criminals to begin using pit bull types as guard dogs, despite the fact that they make terrible guards

---

ACROSS Since Hurricane Katrina and the Michael Vick case, the public has begun to see pit bulls as victims rather than perpetrators.

(pit bulls are often easily stolen), as well as breeding and selling them for large amounts of money based on this new reputation.

From there, it seemed anyone who thought they could make a buck off the cliché of the snarling pit bull began to find ways to capitalize on this new image of the dog. In a notorious July 1987 *Sports Illustrated* cover story, the words "BEWARE OF THIS DOG" were blared in bold letters above the snarling face of . . . well, it was hard to tell if the dog pictured even was any type of pit bull. But the story inside made it clear that the pit bull was the dog to fear, the one who might come and get any one of us in the middle of the night while we slept.

It must have been a very slow week for sports.

In Oklahoma, we spent a day with twelve dogs who were victims not just of dogfighting, but of the public perception of them as well. We took them out one at a time, and then in pairs, cautiously pushing them to see how well they would respond to life outside a cage. What most people don't understand is that in any group of fighting dogs, there may be only a few that have been

fought. The rest of the dogs are excess stock, kept for breeding or selling. In this particular group, Annie and Daisy were among the mama dogs, and as soon as we let two adolescent puppies out of their kennel, they ran straight to Annie to kiss her through the chain-link fence. It was only the twelfth dog, a huge black pit bull at the end of the row, who had obviously been fought. Scars show easily on black dogs, and he was covered with them. When I opened his kennel door, instead of running, he stepped out only far enough to sit at my feet, lean into me, and look up, hoping to be caressed.

Just a few years earlier, these dogs would have been held for evidence and then euthanized without evaluation. But everyone who knows pit bulls knows that they are as resilient as they are sensitive. It isn't surprising, then, that it took surviving a few catastrophes for pit bulls to turn around the misguided public perception of them.

LEFT Pit bulls are becoming belles of the ball in some communities.

ACROSS Despite the myths, most pit bulls are—and have been—the cherished pets of responsible and loving owners.

KATRINA

In August and September of 2005, the city of New Orleans flooded twice following Hurricanes Katrina and Rita and the failure of the U.S. Marine Corps' levee system built to protect the low-lying city. As the citizens evacuated via car or helicopter, thousands of animals were left behind. While the displaced residents (I was one of them) could not return for at least a month (and for most, much longer than that), volunteers began streaming in to help evacuate the animals, and they were surprised by what they found. "Why are there so many pit bulls?"

The Louisiana SPCA estimated that at least 62 percent of the animals rescued post-Katrina were pit bull–type dogs—not 62 percent of all dogs, but of all species of animal. Some rescuers who had never been to New Orleans before were startled by the remnants of extreme poverty that they found surrounded by floodwaters. There was storm damage, of course, but the houses seemed beyond repair even in the unflooded parts of town, and on the front stoops and attic dormers there were pit bulls. To these rescuers, it must have seemed that the pit bulls were of little value to their owners.

But New Orleans has always been characterized by its weathered houses and its pit bull population, which still today is estimated to be at least 50 to 70 percent of all dogs in the city. Poverty is one reason. Pit bull puppies are thought to fetch up to $1,000 apiece (or

---

ACROSS Katrina rescuers were surprised to find so many pit bulls in the flooded city.

even $7,000, according to some), so backyard breeding is common, even if the puppies often end up unsold. (In 2011, the Louisiana SPCA took in 1,667 pit bulls and found homes for just 123.) And in neighborhoods where crime is high and police are rare, having a pit bull in the yard is viewed as an essential form of security system, more for their reputation than for their actual guarding abilities. And more than either of those reasons, people in New Orleans own pit bulls because it has been the chosen family pet for generations.

Many of the rescuers who came from all over the country had never interacted with the breed. And some didn't want to—until they saw the wagging tails, the kissing tongues, and the dancing hips. Pit bulls spotted the rescue boats and dived into the water, trusting completely that they were there to help. Others clung stubbornly to their property, certain that their owners were coming home. The rescuers realized that pit bulls are just dogs after all—although perhaps a little more special than the rest.

Donna Reynolds, the executive director of BAD RAP in Oakland, was on the ground, and remembers how

Annie and Daisy

At the shelter outside Tulsa, we looked to find a soft dog right away, so we could safely assess how the others responded in the presence of a passive dog.

Daisy and Annie, the two mama dogs that we had numbered three and four, were the first to come out. Daisy was lanky and yellow, with a delicate, round head. Annie was smaller, thicker, and red. The staff at the shelter had been unsure what to do with them, so none of the dogs had been outside during the weeks they had stayed there. Sunlight and green grass stunned them for a moment, and then they began prancing and playing as much as their leads would allow. They collapsed at our feet for belly rubs and climbed into our laps and gave each other quick kisses on the mouth.

Once the evaluations were completed, we had to wait for the court to officially release custody before we could place them in rescues; I offered to take Annie to New Orleans, where I could foster her in my home. A few weeks later a transport was arranged. I met her at a sandwich shop in Jackson, Mississippi, and then let her share my turkey-and-avocado sandwich as we drove home. After her first bite of the sandwich, she looked up at me and directly into my eyes, as if she understood for the first time that life was going to change.

After a few days of settling into life in a house, I decided to take her shopping. We stopped in at a fancy dog boutique and she eyed all the stuffed animals gathered on the shelves. After a moment of consideration, she pulled a stuffed dog off the bottom shelf and stepped into its spot. She was very satisfied to be snuggled against the other stuffed animals there.

Several months later, we were preparing to take photos for the Sula Foundation's annual calendar, and we returned to the shop to do her first professional photo shoot. By this time, she had been spayed and had fourteen teeth removed. She probably didn't know what to expect next. The camera and the attention made her nervous. She was afraid to look up, making it difficult to get a good shot of this little dog.

There was a stack of expensive dog beds, about four feet tall, so I lifted her up and placed her carefully in the top bed. She seemed uncertain, then settled into the bed, looked up at the camera, and smiled.

By December she was out at the Saturday market on Freret Street. A volunteer texted me to say, "She's wonderful with children!" Of course she was, I thought; her only job so far in life was to be a mom.

In January 2009, she moved across the river to her new family; the first thing they did was take her on a family vacation to meet her relatives. Most days she spends napping in her crate, or jogging with her dad, and at night she curls up on the bed of one child for a while, then moves to the next room to watch over the other, and then, when she's sure everyone is safe, she goes back to her own bed.

Daisy was adopted by Jeanne and Neil Nutter, who have considered pit bulls a part of their family since their marriage in 1969. After eight wonderful pits that they raised together from puppies, Jeanne and Neil began looking for an adult to adopt after their last dog passed in 2008. "We're too old for puppies," Jeanne says with a laugh.

Neil had his first pit bull in 1947 at the age of eleven. He lived in an area where people were known to fight cocks and dogs, but he never associated those dogs with the one who lived in his home. "I didn't give it much thought," he admits. "That would have broken my heart."

Jeanne hadn't had any experience with the breed until she started dating Neil, which meant she was also dating his pit bull, Pooch, a dark brindle girl who was about seven when they met. "She reminded me of Petey from *The Little Rascals*," Jeanne says. "She was so bright and so well trained."

Because they've owned them for more than four decades, Jeanne and Neil have seen the shifting attitudes toward pit bulls over the years. "It's gotten worse because the media have gotten worse," Jeanne says.

When they picked Daisy, they were looking for a dog that would be a breed ambassador, a member of the family, as well as an active part of the community where they live. When they went to one of BAD RAP's weekend training classes, Daisy ran straight into their arms. "She picked us," they say. "We take her everywhere we go. We make sure people see what a real pit bull is."

PAGE 80 Daisy joins Jeanne Nutter for an afternoon drive.

RIGHT Annie put on her best smile when photographed atop a throne of dog beds.

the tragedy unexpectedly transformed other rescuers' notions about the dogs.

"Hurricane Katrina may have been the first time animal lovers from around the country encountered pit bulls on such a grand scale," she says. "Thousands of volunteer caregivers poured in to flooded communities to help the displaced pets, not realizing that the most popular dog in that part of the country was going to be the pit bull. They encountered hundreds and hundreds of pit bulls stranded on rooftops or already rescued and waiting for care in makeshift triage centers. Suddenly, the mythically frightening beasts were just dogs who needed help, mostly friendly dogs at that. That experience challenged the previous assumptions many held about the breed, and it ignited a new wave of compassion for the dogs."

After the rescues, dogs were shipped across the country, so that they might find homes or find shelter until their owners were located. Thus, the pit bull

---

RIGHT There are few sights so endearing as that of a pit bull puppy face.

survivors began their own diaspora. Just as New Orleanians were displaced across the country and began to introduce their new neighbors to the food and culture of the city, so the New Orleans pit bulls became ambassadors for their breed.

Annabelle, or AnnaBee, was one of these dogs. After being pulled from the streets, she was transferred to a New Mexico shelter, but after three months the shelter was no longer able to save space for these extra dogs in addition to those coming in from their own community.

"We nicknamed her the Hurricane," says Maureen Murray, who adopted her, "because she had a way of barging into a room and turning it upside down. She lived like there was no tomorrow." When brain cancer cut Annabelle's life short at the age of four, Maureen was determined to find a way to keep her spirit around. First came AnnaBee's Doggie Boutique & Cafe, with a view of the Pacifica beaches on which AnnaBee loved to play. Next came Club AnnaBee, a luxury dog hotel,

---

as well as AnnaBee's dog treats, and the Annabelle Foundation, which gives back to the rescue communities who saved her and others like her.

"We miss her so bad you don't even know," Maureen says. "The only way we know how to survive without her is to keep her spirit alive."

THE VICK DOGS

When Michael Vick was arrested on dogfighting charges in July 2007, many people weren't even certain it was news. He was a ballplayer. The dogs were pit bulls, supposedly born to fight, unsalvageable and unlovable. Even the Humane Society of the United States and PETA suggested that the remaining dogs be killed. Others suggested that Vick was being singled out, because of his celebrity or his race. Yet the evidence suggested that what happened to the dogs on Michael Vick's property went beyond mere dogfighting. The dogs were stored in a building at the rear of the property with blacked-out windows. The swimming pool foundation was worn down from dogs trying to claw their way up before being killed by electrocution. Vick admitted to

participating in the torture and deaths of six to eight of the dogs. He couldn't recall the details.

The first problem with dogfighting is that it is morally despicable. The other is that violence toward and abuse of animals, particularly when turned into entertainment, desensitize the participants and drastically increase the likelihood of their committing violence against humans as well. This isn't a strange new theory. It is a long-accepted tenet that has been documented time and time again. The FBI includes the abuse of animals as part of its profiling of serial killers; a number of studies have consistently shown a connection between spousal and child abuse and violence against pets in the home. And yet, because of Vick's celebrity, otherwise reasonable people came running to his defense.

"What did Michael Vick do that is morally reprehensible?" Tulane University sociology professor Shayne

LEFT For better or for worse, dogs are dogs.

ACROSS Two rescued Vick dogs exchange kisses.

Lee wrote in an editorial in the *Philadelphia Inquirer*. "Some of us forget that dogs are mere animals, and that animal mistreatment is as American as Apple iPods. Like Vick, most of us shamelessly abuse and kill animals—for science, leather jackets, ham sandwiches, or horseracing," he wrote, ignoring the fact that in Vick's case, the killing itself was done as a form of entertainment. In writing his editorial, Lee wasn't just voicing his own opinion, he was echoing the thoughts and feelings of many people who had been misled to believe that pit bulls deserved their abuse.

Then a curious thing happened: The public began to ask what would happen to the dogs. Pit bull advocates, bolstered by the bonds they had built saving the dogs of New Orleans, teamed together to push for the opportunity to evaluate each of the Vick dogs as individuals. Two organizations, Best Friends Animal Society and BAD RAP, took the lead in agreeing to take Vick's dogs into their programs, along with additional rescue organizations including the Georgia SPCA, All or Nothing Rescue, Our Pack, Richmond Animal League, Recycled Love, Animal Farm Foundation, the SPCA of Monterey, Out of the Pits, and Animal Rescue of Tidewater.

In a shock to both the public and the rescuers, the evaluations found only two dogs that needed to be euthanized due to behavior. The others were placed with rescue groups across the country, and many of them thrived in the care of their new handlers, earning Canine Good Citizen certificates, obtaining certification as therapy dogs, making public appearances, and even inspiring children's books. They also managed to find homes, with some doing what rescued pit bulls often do: convincing their foster homes to never give them up.

Sports Illustrated, which had contributed to the sensationalizing of the dangerous dog decades earlier, did a cover story on the Vick case. But instead of focusing on Vick, they chose to tell the story of the dogs. "The Bad Newz case was really the first widespread example of dogs recovered from a fight bust being viewed as

ACROSS Otis, another pit bull whose foster family couldn't give him up, is seen on the beach near his family's home.

victims in a crime rather than accomplices," says Jim Gorant, the *Sports Illustrated* reporter whose cover story was later expanded into the book *The Lost Dogs*. "I went into *The Lost Dogs* knowing almost nothing about pit bulls. Really, only what you read in the headlines. Now, I understand that they're simply dogs, and like all dogs they

Uba

Uba really just wants to be a regular dog. A compact black pit bull—old-school variety—Uba loves to play, loves to kiss, and likes to think of himself as a lapdog. But Uba is also carrying a heavy burden, because of the person who owned him before he met his current owner, Letti de Little.

On April 25, 2007, Uba was among fifty-five dogs found in isolation in a windowless kennel on Michael Vick's property in rural Virginia. By September 7, he'd made the *New York Times*, with his photo running in an article headlined "Menacing Dogs from Vick Case Await Their Fate." In the story, the chief animal control officer for Hanover County was quoted as saying, "You don't take two out at the same time; they would just start going at each other."

Yet here is Uba, lying in the sun, relaxing with the family cat and another dog, Lulu.

Letti, his owner, is a sharp young woman, a lawyer born in England, raised in Virginia, and educated in New Orleans. It was her mother, a real-estate agent, who had the first pit bull in the family, a "black Lab mix," according to the shelter. "My mother just wanted a dog," Letti says. "She didn't really care what breed it was."

Later, working in New York City, Letti rescued a chocolate Lab that had been abandoned in his yard.

Then Lulu, a pit bull, came to keep Hershey company, and eventually they settled together in the Bay Area, in a Victorian home in a slightly scrappy neighborhood, one of the few places left where one can still have a yard. When the news broke of the Vick case, and that BAD RAP was taking some of the dogs, Letti felt compelled to volunteer.

"Bringing a dog home from a fight bust, I expected him to be a little bit of a tough guy," she says. "But instead he was soft and sweet and shy." People ask about Uba because they want to know what a "Vick dog" is like. But Uba is Uba, an individual, not a statistic.

"He's taught me more than I've taught him," Letti says. "He's taught me about acceptance." He has also helped her learn to adjust her expectations.

"He doesn't like neighborhood walks," she says. "They terrify him." For a while, Letti kept trying to find ways of working Uba through this issue, and then she realized that she simply needed to respect his needs. What does it matter if he doesn't want to go out on walks? There's the house, and the cat, and the sun just waiting for him, at home.

ACROSS Letti and Uba relax at home.

have the potential for good and bad. They have needs, and may not be for everyone, but if they are socialized properly and trained and managed appropriately, they're generally great dogs."

Gorant's cover story inspired readers to flood the *Sports Illustrated* offices with 488 letters and e-mails— nearly all of the comments positive—the most of any story that year.

Sports Illustrated isn't the only publication to find that a positive story about pit bulls holds more appeal than the negative. At *Bark* magazine, a smart, upscale magazine for dog owners, "a pit bull cover garners more positive comments than any other breed or mix," says publisher Cameron Woo. "Based on the feedback we receive—it tells us that there are more people rooting for pits than any other breed, and they acknowledge and champion all efforts by the media to cast the often maligned breed in a positive light. That's something we constantly try to do—simply to show pits in a neutral or positive light for the dogs that they are . . . loving, obedient, playful, extraordinary."

But perhaps the most obvious sign that the dog days are over for pit bulls may be their emergence as the must-have accessory in advertisements for everything from casual clothes to community banking. Old Navy. The Gap. Lowe's. Martha Stewart. All have chosen to represent their products with a pit bull.

Often the pit bull model has connections. The logo for Plugg jeans features the likeness of the designer's pit bull dog. A television spot for Amazon's Kindle reader demonstrates how lickable the new product is, thanks to a pit bull who lives with one of the commercial's directors. Can the dog take credit for eight million units sold? When Ugg asked quarterback Tom Brady to model their shoes in a Super Bowl ad, he was sure to bring along his pit bull, Lua.

This sudden recognition of the pit bull's appeal isn't really something new. It is a return to another of the dog's traditional roles in American culture. Back at the turn of the century, Buster Brown's pit bull, Tige, was used to sell children's clothing; and other pit bull–type dogs were featured on sheet music, starched collars, perfume, bread, and nearly anything offered for sale.

ACROSS More than twenty years after the original *Sports Illustrated* article cemented pit bulls' reputation as dangerous dogs, Jim Gorant's article helped usher in a new era for pit bulls.

RIGHT Pit bulls are again turning up in advertising. Years ago, they were common "spokesdogs."

MODEL NO. F-335

For Boys   For Girls
BUSTER BROWN
—A BROWN BILT SHOE

MILLIONS of boys and girls are proud to wear Buster Brown Shoes — because they look so neat and are so easy on the feet.

Millions of fathers and mothers buy Buster Brown Shoes for their children—because they know these shoes keep growing feet shapely and make them strong and sturdy—free from corns, bunions, weak ankles, twisted toes and broken arches.

Buster Brown Shoes have Goodyear Welt construction and are made upon the celebrated Brown Shaping Lasts, faithfully following Nature's graceful lines, and giving needed support and protection to each bone and muscle in the feet.

They are made in both low and high cuts—and are sold at $4.00, $5.00, $6.00 and up, according to size and style.

The Brown Shaping Lasts are built upon eighteen scientific measurements, which insure perfect foot protection. The Brown Shaping Lasts provide exactly the correct space inside these shoes for proper growth and development.

Brownbilt Shoes are manufactured only by
Brown Shoe Company, St. Louis, U. S. A.

Advertisers are in the business of pairing their products with images that make people feel good and reflect the values of their community. In returning to the pit bull as spokesdog, advertisers are finally acknowledging again the pit bull's true role as an American family dog.

RIGHT Pit bulls are once again being associated with a positive message.

The Mythology of the Fighting Dog

Who fights a dog? Recent cases suggest there isn't any particular type of dogfighter. Men are joined by women in the so-called sport; their day jobs include teaching children, working at hospitals, just about anything.

Dogfighting has been around for as long as there have been humans and dogs, although it seems a strange occurrence given the intimate, symbiotic, and respectful relationship most of us have with our dogs (and our dogs have with us).

A dogfight is a spectator sport, in which men (and women) gather to watch two dogs square off in a ring. There is usually a pool of money involved, which can be hundreds or even thousands of dollars. But mostly there is a lot of ego and misplaced identity riding on the dogs. The owners feel a sense of worth in proportion to their dogs' success in the ring, the same way the rest of us root for a football team.

There are stories of dogs fighting to the death, but more likely the scene plays out like a boxing match or bad professional wrestling. The match can be called when the winner is apparent, so that he or she can then go on to fight again. Pit bulls, with their athletic bodies and acrobatic moves, were found to make great pawns in this game.

Contrary to widely accepted mythology, the dogs don't particularly like fighting. They fight because they are forced to, and they have little choice about the matter. Sometimes the losing dog is abandoned, or subjected to further abuse. And the existence of this barbaric sport has no correlation to how an individual dog might act outside the ring. Often, the most scarred survivors are also the gentlest with people.

The machismo of the dogfighting scene eventually led people—the wrong people—to seek out the pit bull as an emblem of danger or protection, and the public began to reverse the cause-effect relationship in the equation. The bad guys in movies could be established quickly by the presence of a snarling pit bull. The machismo of a rapper in a video was made clear by a spike-collared, big-headed pit at their side. And on No Trespassing signs—why not add a pit bull?

With all these emblems of danger burned into our minds, it was inevitable that some people would get confused and think that the dogs were inspiring bad behavior among the people, instead of the reality, which is that it was the other way around.

ACROSS This dog, rescued from a dogfighting operation, is finally being seen as a victim, not a perpetrator.

pits in the
community

ON MARCH 19, 2007, A PIT BULL WAS HIT BY A VAN driving through Hoboken, New Jersey. On the face of it, this event was not particularly remarkable—especially with the pit bull populations being as high as they are, coupled with the number of them allowed to roam stray and the number of drivers who don't particularly care to stop when a ten-year-old brindle dog, wearing a T-shirt for warmth, runs in front of their car. But the story of Foxy is a story of community.

LEFT Pit bulls are increasingly being seen as benevolent members of communities throughout the United States.

Foxy's owner was a homeless man named Randy Vargas, and they were a familiar sight in the neighborhood. In fact, the people who passed them each day were so moved by the bond between these two creatures, man and pit bull, that when Vargas was briefly jailed and Foxy sent to the pound, a local groomer went to collect her, saving her from euthanasia and returning her to Vargas when he was released.

So when Foxy was struck down, and Vargas ran to the animal hospital carrying her in his arms, and the news spread that Foxy didn't make it, the neighborhood was brought together in an unexpected, inspiring jolt of mourning. Shops posted photos of Foxy in memorial; strangers donated money so that Vargas could one day get a new dog. And strangest of all, the *New York Times* wrote an incredibly moving tribute to this homeless man and his dog:

"Maybe in a world of opaque relationships, theirs was a lesson in clarity like a parable from the Bible. He had rescued her back when she was homeless and abused, a scared runty thing living with homeless men who had no use for her. She in turn gave him purpose and companionship and love."

Peter Applebome, the reporter who filed the story, wasn't entirely surprised at the enormous reader response that followed.

"In the seven and a half years I did the column, I'd say it was one of the two most popular columns I did," he recalls. "It got a huge response—all positive. I'm not sure I expected to find the metaphor for life in Hoboken, but I'm a sucker for dog stories. I have a sixteen-year-old Corgi/something else mix (he's been described as half a dog high and two dogs long) who is a huge part of my life, so the idea instantly resonated."

WORKING DOGS

The bond between dogs and people has been established through history, as dogs have served their masters as companions, hunters, guide dogs, and even have been trained to work as officers of the law. (A canine officer killed in the line of duty is treated to the same honors and observances as a human officer.) Yet people who

---

ACROSS After Foxy's death, this photo became a memorial to her throughout the neighborhood—and in the *New York Times*.

don't know pit bulls are often surprised to find that they are working dogs, too. Pit bulls are found working as detection dogs for U.S. Customs, the Washington State Patrol and Washington State Ferries System, and for local police departments throughout the country. Dogs are dogs, but the media's representation of pit bull–type dogs as being almost a separate species leaves some people unprepared to see them contributing to the community.

But pit bulls are hard workers, dedicated to completing the task at hand, even if for some of them their biggest contribution to the community is in taking long naps on the couch. Increasingly, pit bulls are entering the working world, due to their intelligence, their dedication, and their capacity to learn complicated tasks.

All of these characteristics, combined with their portable size, have made them increasingly attractive

LEFT Pit bulls make great therapy dogs for literacy programs, providing a nonjudgmental ear for struggling readers.

ACROSS As with most dogs, a pit bull can make a great companion for almost anyone, at any age.

102

as service dogs and as therapy dogs. Pit bulls can fit in small spaces and easily travel by car or by plane. And, of course, having pit bulls contributing to the community (visiting hospitals, literacy programs, and doing police

work) is a great way to introduce the breed to people who might have otherwise looked the other way.

When Marthina McClay, the founder of Our Pack, a pit bull rescue organization, was a child, her family

The Mystery of Helen Keller's Pit Bull

Helen Keller had a pit bull. This is a statement that can be found on any number of pit bull websites, sometimes accompanied by a small black-and-white photo of a woman sitting next to a nearly unidentifiable blob of a dog. It could be a pit bull, or maybe some kind of hound. Aside from the dog's name, Sir Thomas, there doesn't appear to be much anyone has to say about him, or how he was acquired, or, perhaps most important, how Helen Keller felt about this dog.

Helen Keller was left deaf and blind after an illness in infancy, and her struggle to learn how to interact with the world was the basis for many books, as well as the popular stage play and film adaptation *The Miracle Worker*. If she had a pit bull, it might well have been one of the first therapy dogs in history. So why was there no record of Sir Thomas, even in Keller's own memoirs and essays?

If there was evidence that Sir Thomas was a pit bull, and that Helen loved him, I wanted to know. But if it was all hearsay, I didn't want to contribute to the mythology. There

---

LEFT Helen Keller is shown with her dog Phiz, aka Sir Thomas.

are enough rumors spread about pit bulls. We didn't need another one, even if it was positive in its intent.

I made a phone call to the American Foundation for the Blind's Helen Keller archive and left a message on their voice mail. "I'm looking for information on one of Helen's dogs, Sir Thomas," I explained, knowing better than to expect anyone to get back in touch with the answer to such an odd request. Yet, the next day, my cell rang as I sat down for morning coffee. "You're looking for information on Sir Thomas?" the woman asked.

"Yes!" I answered.

"We don't have any reference to a Sir Thomas," she said, crushing my hopes, "but she did write a lot about her dogs, particularly one called Phiz."

"Was he a pit bull?" I asked hopefully.

"I don't think so," the woman replied. And then I decided to come clean: I was looking for something that would confirm the existence of Sir Thomas, and that he was a pit bull–type dog.

"We usually charge for this kind of thing," she said. "But I can take another look."

Fifteen minutes later she called. "It turns out Phiz and Sir Thomas were the same dog."

In photos of the two of them together, Phiz looks like a small, compact, old-school pit bull, though somewhat shortchanged in the snout department. Helen holds him close, their faces next to each other in one posed shot. In another, Phiz is sprawled at her feet with his head turned properly toward the camera. In correspondence from the breeder's son to the vice president of Radcliffe College, "Tom" is described as an "oversized" Boston terrier, a breed that had been established with the AKC just ten years before Helen's classmates decided to purchase Tom as a gift.

Soon Tom was dubbed Sir Thomas, and then (like many of our dogs) he took on another, more particular, nickname: Phiz. But whether he was a small pit bull or a giant Boston terrier (essentially the same thing; Boston terriers are bred-down bull and terrier mixes), all that mattered to Helen was that Phiz was Phiz. "His boundless good nature, his readiness to be friends with everybody, and his mirth-provoking antics won the favor of all who were wise in the ways of bull terriers," she wrote.

In *The Story of My Life*, she noted, "I have had many dog friends—huge mastiffs, soft-eyed spaniels, wood-wise setters and honest, homely bull terriers. At present the lord of my affections is one of these bull terriers. He has a long pedigree, a crooked tail and the drollest 'phiz' in dogdom. My dog friends seem to understand my limitations, and always keep close beside me when I am alone. I love their affectionate ways and the eloquent wag of their tails."

kept shepherds and Dobermans. "They may as well have been spawned from the devil," she says now, referring not to their actual behavior, but to the popular myths of the time regarding both breeds. So she was used to judging animals as individuals by the time she began doing training work—first with horses, and later, inevitably, with dogs.

Her first therapy dog, a pit bull named Hailey, met some resistance from hospitals and nursing homes because of her breed. But after several interviews with skeptical administrators, Hailey and Marthina finally found an administrator with an open mind about the breed. Looking over Hailey's paperwork, he said, "She has more certificates than I do, and *I went to college.*"

As a trainer, Marthina had noticed an interesting problem with pit bulls. Many of their owners anticipated behavioral issues, and through their own inadvertent actions encouraged those behaviors. Then, rather than correcting them, they simply gave up on the idea of directing their dogs' behavior, because they had been told that they could not.

"They were told to expect their dogs to misbehave," she says—by the media, by their neighbors, by people who knew nothing about dogs in general or the particular dog in question. Of the dogs she saw with true issues, they were rarely pit bulls.

Inspired by Hailey, and the problems that pit bull owners so often anticipated, Marthina set herself a

---

ACROSS Pit bulls, like other dogs, have been shown to lower blood pressure in patients—and their owners.

mission of changing the way the breed was perceived, through training and work in the community.

Hailey had a favorite patient who had MS. She would lie next to her twice a week and the woman would talk to Hailey about all the dogs she'd had in her life, before being hospitalized. And as she spoke about her dogs, she would begin to speak more clearly. This is one of the most effective aspects of therapy work with dogs—they connect to patients who can recall the joy their own pets brought them, no matter how long ago they may have been in the past.

But as much as Marthina loved working with Hailey, it was Leo who really stole her heart. Leo was one of Michael Vick's dogs, and Marthina had him certified as a therapy dog within five weeks of taking custody.

"I've worked with hundreds of dogs. People are drawn to Leo. I've never had a dog that was so magnetic. When he came to me, I was prepared for anything. But I never realized I would be meeting the Casanova of dogs. He has this way of romancing you with those brown eyes of his—he's truly amazing." Like all therapy dogs, Leo liked cuddling and hugs,

Bud

On May 23, 1903, Vermont physician Horatio Nelson Jackson set off with a chauffeur named Sewall Crocker and a used Winton, dubbed the Vermont, to prove it was possible to drive a car coast to coast.

It seems fitting that the first cross-country car ride was hijacked by a pit bull named Bud. Pit bulls love cars almost as much as they love people—and what better way to meet new people and be forced to snuggle closely than a sixty-three-day trip in an early model car. Stories claim that Bud joined the trip after chasing the car for two miles, but in a letter to his wife, Jackson explained that he had left his coat behind at a hotel stop and "on our way back, we were stopped by a man and asked if I didn't want a dog for a mascot." And thus Bud became the third party in this history-making expedition. When they quickly discovered that his eyes were sensitive to the dust of unpaved roads, they assembled a custom pair of driving goggles for Bud, which he wore for the rest of the trip. Bud learned to anticipate and brace himself for the many bumps in the road, although one unexpected piece of road debris sent all three passengers airborne.

In photographs from the trip, Bud is often perched riding confidently in the shotgun seat—and just as often patrolling alongside the stalled car while they waited for repairs. Bud, like so many pit bulls, was a total media hound, and soon he began racking up as many headlines as Jackson and the road trip itself. The New York papers were particularly taken with him, even though—or perhaps because—by that time he was refusing all interviews. He was, Jackson claimed, "the one member of the trio who used no profanity on the trip."

When the fanfare was over, Bud joined Jackson and his wife to lead a quiet life in Vermont.

ABOVE Horatio Nelson Jackson and Bud are pictured together.

and was dedicated to just making people feel right. The EMTs at one local hospital began calling him Dr. Leo. Most of us know what it's like to settle in with our own dogs, the way that they know us and when we need them at our side, how they can sense when to press extra close and when to play a joke. Leo had that sense about everyone, even if they had never previously met.

Together they were featured in numerous newspapers, magazines, and television shows. They were a team. In December 2011, four years after being rescued, Leo passed away after suffering from a seizure disorder. It is still hard for Marthina to talk about him in the past tense.

"Leo was just who he was, that's what made him beautiful. I just provided an environment that allowed him to be himself."

PIT BULLS: A HISTORY IN SERVICE

For generations, pit bulls' sturdy dignity qualified them as great family dogs, service dogs, and military

RIGHT Marthina is still adjusting to life without Leo.

DOG "JACK,"

*Attached to the 102d Regiment Pennsylvania Vols.,
was in the following Battles:*

Siege of Yorktown; Battle of Williamsburg; Fair Oaks;
Battle of the Pickets; Malvern Hill, (wounded;) First and
Second Fredericksburg; Captured at Salem Church, was
exchanged and returned.

heroes. During the U.S. Civil War, there were at least two pit bulls that served as honored members of the military: Jack served in the Union army with the 102nd Regiment, and was so valued by his unit that when he was captured by the Confederates, the soldiers negotiated the exchange of a Confederate soldier in order to assure his safe return. Sallie, a brindle girl who served with the Eleventh Pennsylvania Volunteer Infantry, was separated from her battalion during a battle, but was later found guarding the dead and wounded. Sallie was later struck by a bullet and died at Hatcher's Run in 1865. Unlike military dogs today, the dogs brought to battle during the Civil War were family pets, accompanying their masters in their call to duty.

Later, during World War I, it was the pit bull, then called the American bull terrier, who was featured on

LEFT Jack was a pit bull who served with the Union army during the Civil War.

ACROSS Pit bulls were used to represent the United States before and during World War I.

I'm Neutral, BUT—Not Afraid
of any of them.

English Bulldog

German Dachshund

American Bull Terrier

French Bulldog

Russian Wolf-Hound

WALLACE ROBINSON—1915

U.S. propaganda posters, representing the country's position: neutral, but prepared to join the fight. "I'm Neutral, BUT—Not Afraid of any of them," is the caption beneath one panel, with the proud pit bull in the center, surrounded by dogs representing other countries. Another shows a pit bull guarding a litter of kittens nestled on the American flag: "Safe," it reads, "under the right protection." The image of a pit bull is also featured on postcards of the time, and on many you can find notes from soldiers writing home from the front lines of the war that ended in 1918.

Pit bulls also served in battle during World War I. Sergeant Stubby was a stray pit bull mix that was smuggled by soldiers to France. Prior to their deployment, Stubby had trained alongside the men, and he had even learned to mimic their salute by raising his right paw to his brow. In Europe, he saved troops by warning them of an incoming gas attack. He also managed to capture a German spy, after which he became the only dog promoted to sergeant. Among the many medals awarded to him was the Purple Heart.

PIT BULLS IN SERVICE

Although pit bulls served on the front lines of the Civil War and the first and second World Wars, today's pit bulls remain at home waiting for their soldier's return, alongside the husbands, wives, and children who are left safely behind. It is here that the dogs have found yet another role they can fulfill, providing emotional support for loved ones and helping veterans overcome the effects of post-traumatic stress when they return.

Post-traumatic stress, or PTSD, is increasingly seen in survivors of violence on the battlefield. Those who suffer from it are caught in their own head, reliving the trauma, waking in the middle of the night, exploding in unpredictable emotional outbursts, or filled with self-doubt. These behaviors are compounded for many in the military because they feel they cannot share what they are going through without their records being tarnished.

When David Sharpe found himself at rock bottom, sitting with a pistol in his mouth and ready to pull the trigger, it was his six-month-old pit bull, Cheyenne, that snapped him out of it—by licking his ear and looking at him quizzically. In an interview with the *Washington Post*, Sharpe said, "It was like 'What are you doing? Who's going to take care of me? Who else is going to let me sleep in this bed?'"

Not only did Cheyenne give Sharpe something to live for, she also provided him a nonjudgmental ear. When his family didn't or couldn't understand what he was going through, she was there.

David went on to found Pets4Vets.org, an organization that works to match abandoned animals with veterans to provide emotional support as they recover from the trauma of their experiences.

The pit bull's most treasured role, however, has been its place as a family dog for more than a century—in other words, for as long as the breed has been known to exist. Some say the dog was known as the Victorian-era "nanny dog" trusted to look after children when the parents were away, but there is little evidence to suggest that anyone of the time used this term. What

ACROSS Many dogs, including pit bulls, were seen on the battlefields during World War I and World War II.

RIGHT An early photo shows a pit bull in its most cherished role: children's companion.

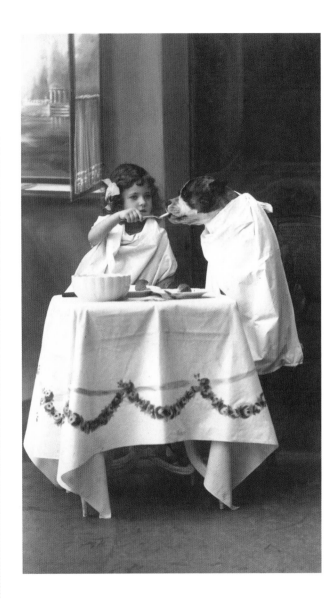

is clear, from countless old black-and-white photos and tintypes, is that the pit bull–type dog was considered a part of the family. There was nothing unusual about having one or two lounging on the lawn, or in early snapshots of family gatherings, and certainly nothing unusual about inviting them to join you for a drive in the car as Bud joined Horatio Jackson in his historic car ride across the country.

And Bud wasn't alone in the papers. Aunt Jane's Letter Club in the *New Orleans Times-Picayune* published a letter in 1933 from a child's pit bull, asking, "May dogs become members of your club?" (The answer, of course, was yes.) This pit bull, named Bullie, went on to admit that he liked to bark, and explained in his letter that "for dogs, barking is a pleasure, as singing is to people."

The history of the pit bull winds its way through the history of our own country in a way that makes it seem impossible to pull them apart.

SPORTING ACES

Pit bulls are also found competing in all types of canine sports. Their natural athleticism, drive, and intelligence make them ideal participants in everything from agility to flyball to weight pulling to dock jumping. There are even pit bull types who are joining their smaller terrier cousins in the sport of going-to-ground (chasing the scent of a rodent through an earthen tunnel).

Wallace was a two-year-old pit bull being fostered in a family of athletes when his natural abilities first became known. "I've been an athlete all my life, so I enjoyed being able to work in competitive sports with my dog, too," says Roo Yori, Wallace's former foster dad and current owner. Yes, Wallace is another pit bull foster dog that never had to find another home.

Yori hadn't thought of working with Wallace—it hadn't occurred to him that he would be interested—but one day his wife, Clara, having noticed some dormant desire in their pit bull guest, suggested he give it a try. They borrowed a Frisbee that belonged to Roo's mutt, Ajax, who had competed in some local disc competitions, and headed out into the yard. It took only a few throws for Wallace to catch on. Soon

ACROSS Wallace and Roo show off their moves on the disc field.

Pit Bulls of the Rich and Famous

When met with skepticism about their breed of choice, pit bull owners will often begin reciting a memorized list of famous pit bull owners, as if being famous is some measure for responsible decision-making. Does it really matter what kind of dog the rich and famous are supporting? Not really, but it is nice to point out the instances when those who could choose any dog they want share our good taste. Of course, there were Helen Keller and James Thurber and Teddy Roosevelt and Dr. Seuss, all of whom chose their dogs before pop culture had turned public opinion against them. But more recent additions to the celebrity pit bull hall of fame include many who use their celebrity to advocate on behalf of the breed.

When actor and comedian Mary Tyler Moore published an autobiography a few years ago, every interview she gave seemed to mention her pit bull, Spanky, who is so attuned to her that he is able to alert her when her blood sugar is low. "He can sense when something's not right," she told *People* magazine. "He will come and sit and stare at me until I do something about it."

Moore's friend Broadway musical star Bernadette Peters shares her passion for the breed; in one of her most popular publicity photos, Bernadette and her brindle pit bull, Stella, seem to vie for the title of most glamorous. She's even written a series of children's books about Stella fighting expectations based on her appearance.

Jon Stewart has two pit bulls in his family, and has used *The Daily Show* as a platform to speak of his love for the breed. And sports stars love the breed for its high energy level. Off-season workouts always go better when you have a pit bull partner working at your side as a pacer.

Rachael Ray has a line of dog food that features her pit bull, Isaboo, on the bag, and she has often discussed the virtues of the breed on her daily talk show.

And even soap stars have found themselves beguiled by a pit bull. Cassandra Creech grew up in a small North Carolina town, dreaming of becoming a successful actor. By the time she got to New York City in the 1990s, she knew that finding your path in life was as much about hard work as it was about luck. She had landed roles on two popular soap operas—*Another World* and *As the World Turns*—but it was a call from her neighborhood pet supply store that really changed her life. The staff knew her well from her visits with her golden retriever, Max.

"Cassandra, you have to meet this little girl," they said. "She's very shy and doesn't come out for anyone." Her owner, a homeless man from the neighborhood, had asked them to care for her, because he knew that he no longer could.

So Cassandra walked over to meet Tigerlily. "She was this little brindle pup. I pet her and when I turned and walked away . . . she followed me. That was it. I got a new dog."

Tigerlily had scars on her head and all over her body. She had a smelly rotten tooth and a chunk of her right ear was missing. She was Cassandra's first pit bull, and, as is often the case, it was immediate love.

Though unfamiliar with the breed, Cassandra had a lifelong love of animals, developed particularly after losing her twin sister to cancer at a young age. And the bond she shared with Tigerlily satisfied a part of her that acting did not. She now balances acting with her own dog hiking and training company in Los Angeles.

"It is a wonderful counterbalance," she says. "I am known as the 'Big-Dog Girl.' . . . Each day I take several groups of dogs hiking in the Santa Monica Mountains. It's extraordinary watching the dogs communicate with each other. They train each other. Most times I am the student and 'they' are the teachers."

Tigerlily has passed on, but she left Cassandra with a legacy that balances out the highs and lows of a life in the arts. And that, of course, is one of the best aspects of living with a pit bull, or any other dog. They remind us of what is

really important—it takes more than fancy cars or your name on the list at a club for them to be impressed.

ABOVE Bernadette Peters is seen with her pit bull, Stella.

they were competing in disc competitions, where
dogs and their owners demonstrate their abilities in
distance and freestyle (choreographed, much like a

gymnastic routine) throwing and retrieval. At their
first competition, Wallace was the only pit bull on a
field of border collies and herding dogs. In his first

year competing, Wallace managed to qualify for the UFO and AWI world championships. In 2007, he won the Purina Incredible Dog Challenge Freestyle National Championship.

Wallace was training for the Purina Incredible Dog Challenge National Finals in 2008 when tragedy almost struck: in a burst of excitement (or perhaps it was caused by performance anxiety), Wallace swallowed a rubber kitchen spatula whole. Wallace survived, but the news of his error in judgment quickly made its way into newspapers around the world when Purina, the sponsor of the competition, announced that he would be unable to compete. While the spatula incident was neither planned nor pleasant, it was a typical stroke of pit bull luck—an unfortunate incident that managed to accomplish Roo's goal of putting Wallace (and all pit bulls) in front of the public in a positive light.

"People enjoyed watching him," Roo says. "Even people who didn't like pit bulls thought that it was cool.

___

ACROSS Pit bulls excel in many canine sports, including agility.

It was a whole new way to change people's perception about the breed."

Wallace's competitions weren't limited to disc; he competed in weight pulling, too. In weight pulling, the dogs are harnessed and asked to pull increasing amounts of weight a distance of sixteen feet. They have only one minute to complete the task. No luring is allowed; the dog either chooses to do it, or not. Weight pulling, as you might imagine, is somewhat more controversial than teaching a dog to retrieve a disc, yet it is considered one of the traditional competition sports for the pit bull breeds. The controversy, as always, stems from two things: false assumptions regarding the nature of the sport and a small number of competitors who practice it inhumanely.

"It is kind of a macho thing," Roo says. "But like everything else, if you do it right, it can be great." Wallace, a fifty-pound dog, was able to pull 1,735 pounds on a wheeled car—which was good enough for second place.

Although Wallace is now a senior dog and no longer competes professionally in sports, Roo encourages other

119

pit bull owners to involve their dogs in sports or
other activities; Roo continues to work with Hector,
one of Michael Vick's former dogs; and Wallace is
enjoying his retirement by telling his story in a new

biography by Jim Gorant. "Finding a sport you can do
together is a great way to bond [with your dog] and
stay healthy—and teach people about the breeds,"
says Roo.

THE ART OF THE PIT BULL

Every pit bull is a work of art. Every socked foot and dangling jowl. Every brindle stripe.

In his studio in Oakland, California, Tim Racer is on the three hundredth hour of a 550-hour project: the latest of his carved wooden carousel figures in the form of a pit bull. This is not what he imagined doing when he was in art school in Detroit, nor when he moved with his wife, Donna Reynolds, from Chicago, where they had a lucrative illustration studio, to California two decades ago. There, he stumbled upon a new vocation: restoring antique wooden carousel figures.

Tim comes from a family of tree trimmers, so restoring—and in some cases recarving—sections of carousel figures came naturally to him. But after restoring the work of European master carvers for eight years, he realized that he'd gotten away from his own art.

ACROSS AND RIGHT BAD RAP founders Tim Racer and Donna Reynolds find pit bulls in their mission and their art. Racer carves pit bull carousel figures (across), while Reynolds creates pit bull–inspired folk art (right).

After presenting his restoration work at an annual conference, he decided to challenge himself by promising to return the next year with an original work.

Nobody's done a pit bull carousel figure before, he thought. And he had the perfect inspiration for this new work: his own pit bull Sally, who has struggled against mast cell cancer for years. With both his subject and his deadline set, he set to work on what became the first of many dog portraits, most of them pit bulls. How much do people love their dogs? His commissions range in price from $12,000 to $55,000 apiece. His art is not breed-specific, and everything is life-sized. Still, he admits, "Half of what I do ends up being pit bull art."

His pieces aren't the only amazing pit bull–inspired art decorating the house; there is also the folk art created by his wife, Donna. Of course, it comes as no surprise that these two might find their creative minds drifting toward pit bulls. BAD RAP, the Bay Area pit bull advocacy group that they founded on April Fools'

Day 2001, has become the nation's most prominent pit bull advocacy group. Out on their large property is a newly constructed barn, where volunteers work with the temporary resident pit bulls before sending them on to foster or permanent homes.

Both Tim and Donna love to scour flea markets for great art finds, and when they spotted someone wheeling away a heavy bronze bust of a pit bull, they knew it had to be theirs. Too late, it seemed. Someone had beaten them to it. But somehow Tim finagled a deal to buy the statue back and surprised Donna with it on her July 4 birthday. It is the work of Armenian-born artist Nishan Toor, who produced work beginning in the late 1800s and passed away in 1966. What in the world was he doing creating a life-size sculpture of an American pit bull? Tim Racer's guess: "It had to have been a commission," proving there is nothing new about the sometimes extravagant devotion we show our dogs.

SHOW DOGS

When my mom was still alive, she would send me news clippings in the mail or via e-mail, with no note

ACROSS Pit bulls may be busy, but they also find time to smell the flowers.

The All-American Mascot

Baseball is the all-American sport, so it's no surprise to find more than a few pit bulls sprinkled through its history. While other bat-and-ball games predate it, the sport in the form we know it today began to take hold in the United States in the mid-1850s—just about the same time that the earliest pit bulls began to prove themselves as family pets and battle-field companions. Among the thousands of photos in the archives at Animal Farm Foundation, it's quite remarkable how many of these black-and-white images portray uniformed baseball players, mitts and bats in hand, gathered around the team pit bull.

And it wasn't just baseball teams: there are teams of all kinds gathered around the dogs—basketball, football, women's softball. Even boxer Jack Dempsey chose to spend his time outside the ring with a pit bull. Perhaps it is the dogs' athleticism that appeals to the athletes among us; or maybe it is because, like most athletes, our pit bulls have pushed their way through some rough times with a tenacity that is unwavering. They are capable of inspiring us to push forward too, to reach for the best for them and the best for us.

Even today, more than 135 years after the founding of the National League, baseball players and their pit bulls stand together through whatever challenges come their way. In 2012, when Mark Buehrle signed with the Miami Marlins, many fans wondered what would become of Slater, his family's eighteen-month-old pit bull. With a pit bull ban still in effect in Miami-Dade county when Buehrle signed, he and his wife realized they wouldn't be able to reside in the city where he would now play. Not satisfied to quietly settle out of town, they took the opportunity to go public with their feelings about breed-discriminatory legislation. With a player's salary, they had far more options available to them than most pit bull owners who are forced by law to give up their family pets. In an interview with the *Miami Herald*, Buehrle said, "it's kind of ridiculous that because of the way a dog looks, people will ban it. Every kind of dog has good and bad, and that depends on the handlers . . . Slater would never do anything harmful."

There's an old slang term in baseball: a dirt dog. Dirt dogs are scrappy. Dirt dogs have been around the block. They are hard working, and a bit rough around the edges. They never give up. Not a bad comparison to America's mutt, the pit bull.

ACROSS A 1904 Brooklyn baseball team poses with their pit bull mascot.

or anything to personalize the contents. Whatever connection I might have to an article was meant to be understood without explanation. It was, honestly, an annoying habit. But increasingly, as we both got older, the contents had to do with pit bulls, and in this case, she was right to assume that I would understand what it meant that she had thought to send it on to me.

The headline of the *Pottsville Republican-Herald* article by Andrew Staub read: "Abused Pottsville Pit Bull Lands a Role in 'Oliver!'"

"The injuries that once made potential adopters cringe vaulted a dog named Thanos into local stardom Monday," read the article.

"Thanos, a purebred 4-year-old pit bull from Pottsville, landed the role of villain Bill Sykes' dog in the Performing Arts Institute's production of 'Oliver!', outshining eight other tailed thespians in auditions held at the Wyoming Seminary Upper School campus on North Sprague Avenue on Monday.

"'It wasn't even close,' [director Bill Roudebush] said. 'From the minute he walked on campus, he had the part.' . . . Roudebush needed to find a dog that looked the part of a ruffian junkyard canine but still had a sweet temperament."

I was impressed that this relatively small town in Pennsylvania's coal region was ready to launch a pit bull into musical theater stardom. How had this lucky pup landed on his feet?

Thanos's rescue story begins (and ends) in a rabbit hutch, where he was found alone at three weeks old, his ears cropped by an amateur using fishing line.

Amy Eckert had been volunteering with the Hillsdale SPCA since her freshman year in high school. "Pits rarely came in," she remembers, "but there wasn't that stigma." By the time Thanos showed up in her life, Amy had become a certified trainer, opened a kennel facility, and graduated to working on animal cruelty investigations for the SPCA. Thanos's real name is Brierwood's Not What You Think CD, CDX, RN, RA, RE, CGC, TDI. But most people call him Thanos.

ACROSS When Thanos is not onstage, he does therapy work with his rabbit sibling, Izzy.

"His drives are phenomenal," Amy says. She began working with him immediately on AKC obedience, agility, and rally as a way of teaching him how to direct his drive into fun, productive activities. He's also certified as a therapy dog and spends a great deal of his time visiting schools and nursing homes, often accompanied by his good friend, a bunny rabbit named Izzy.

While Thanos played a part in a musical, another pit bull named Butley took his act on the road,

touring with a production of the award-winning musical *Spring Awakening*. Those familiar with the play, about frustrated passionate teens in the late nineteenth century, might have trouble remembering a role suitable for a dog. Butley's responsibilities were strictly offstage.

Actors Todd Cerveris and Angie Reed adopted Butley from the New York rescue organization Stray from the Heart. Butley came to them via a friend who was fostering the dog but needed someone to fill in while he moved. Angie agreed to take him for a few days, and then a week, and then, while Todd was on tour with *Twelve Angry Men*, she called to let him know that they had just adopted Butley.

Technically an American Staffordshire terrier, Butley was found wandering the Bronx at the age of two. When he arrived in the overcrowded New York Animal Care and Control shelter, he was scheduled to be put down the next day. But the volunteers at the NYACC have a remarkable system in place for finding foster spots in a dog's hour of need. They take photos, write creative descriptions, and network the dogs through the foster system each night. Not all of them make it, but Butley was one of the lucky ones.

A registered service dog, Butley knows how to turn on the charm in almost any situation, whether it's visiting patients in the hospital or encountering construction workers on Manhattan streets. ("Damn, that face!" one

---

ACROSS Angie Reed relaxes with show-stopper Butley.

construction worker recently said. "He don't look like no dog, man—he looks like he's human!")

Naturally, when both Todd and Angie were cast in the *Spring Awakening* tour, there wasn't a chance they would leave him behind. Together, the family traveled twenty-two thousand miles, staying in dog-friendly hotels all along the way.

Even though Butley didn't appear in the show, he still managed to attract his own groupies waiting backstage. "We took a *Spring Awakening* T-shirt and fashioned it for Butley's adornment, so that he could be a 'Guilty One' just like all the other die-hard fans who had decided to name themselves after one of the songs from the show," said Todd.

"At the theaters which allowed us to bring him to visit, he'd sometimes wear his T-shirt, proudly greeting the long lines of fans waiting for autographs and photos of the cast after a performance. Butley soon became the sought-after postshow encounter, and we even caught chatter on the fan website where fans would discuss what a handsome dog we had traveling with us. He never signed any 'paw-tographs,' but he did pose for a

few pictures. And, of course, fans who saw Angie and me leaving after a show would ask us 'Where's Butley?!'

"People would literally stop their cars on the street as they passed by—to talk to him, and to us *about* him. I'm not saying my actor-ego was bruised exactly; but it wasn't lost on me that my dog was more famous than I was!"

For now, Butley has put his stage work on hold for quiet pursuits: breakfast, dinner, and a series of five children's books about the five boroughs of New York City. First up: *Butley from the Bronx*.

DOGS ON PARADE

New Orleans is a city of tradition, and increasingly our traditions include a role for our dogs. In the middle of Carnival season, the Barkus parade clogs traffic in and around the French Quarter as the city's dogs represent their breeds, their families, and their neighborhoods in a parade that lasts most of the afternoon. I may be biased, but each year it seems that our pit bull Krewe

LEFT The pit bull Krewe in New Orleans continues to grow.

Hamsa Sings the Blues

Zach Sharaga was just twenty when he bought Louis 649, a little jazz bar in the East Village of Manhattan, on 9th Street between B and C. The previous owner had been a furniture maker who redid the inside, and was rarely seen without his dog, an old pit bull who mostly found the coolest place to park on the bar floor, or followed the servers when they brought plates of food out to the tables.

Zach knew little of his new bar's dog history when he bought it. He grew up without pets of any kind. But shortly after acquiring the bar, he found a tiny white pit bull puppy while out walking. He'll always remember the day he decided to take the puppy in: it was April Fools' Day.

"I was living alone in the Bronx," Zach says. "Every day I worked at the bar from 11 in the morning 'til 4 the next morning. Hamsa came to work with me every single day. He is my sidekick and is known to every single person to have walked through the door. He's even developed an ear for jazz and now howls along to John Coltrane and Sonny Rollins." It wasn't long before Hamsa became the official face of Louis 649; a portrait of Hamsa serving behind the bar greets anyone who passes on the street.

For someone who never had a pet growing up, the most surprising thing, Zach says, is "how connected we are. Pit bulls have really given me an opportunity to see the range of human nature when encountering them."

RIGHT Hamsa tends bar at Louis 649.

grows larger, and the crowd reaction louder, than any of the other groups. (Okay, I'm really probably not the one to judge.) As our gang of bead-wearing pits rounds each corner, cheers erupt and the children and their parents call out for the prized throws we pitch on behalf of our dogs. There was probably a time when this surprised people—the pit bulls parading down narrow, crowded streets, surrounded by children and other dogs, without incident. But now there's nothing surprising about it. It's become an expectation, a sign that the pit bulls have been welcomed back into the community, as individuals. As equals.

RIGHT Pit bulls are being welcomed back into our communities as well as our homes.

afterword

"HAVING TO SAY GOOD-BYE TO A PIT BULL IS RIGHT
up there with the hardest things I've ever done," Jeanne
Nutter told me. This was the one fault she could find after
loving eight pit bulls. Because pit bulls live their lives so
intensely, so fully, with such a great appreciation for every
moment they are alive, the void they leave behind is made
that much harder to fill.

When I lost my Sula, I wasn't prepared for the hole that
was created in her wake. So much of the rhythm of my life
had been created around her, losing her was like losing a limb.
Writing this book was a way to try to fill that space up again.

LEFT There is nothing like the love
of a pit bull.

When you fall in love with pit bulls, there is no turning back. Who you are changes, because of what they teach you and because of what we need to do to protect them.

Several years ago, I was invited to speak at a national conference outside Denver regarding "dangerous dogs." The topic was a misnomer, because what was really being discussed were pit bulls (and to a lesser extent, Rottweilers), and it seemed most people cared about defending the breed. But there were those in attendance who weren't sure; some came from communities where breed-discriminatory laws had been passed or were in some stage of proposal, ranging from outright bans of the dogs to specific expectations of responsible ownership pertaining to specific breeds.

I was the final speaker, so I listened carefully to what everyone who spoke before me had to say, so that I could be sure to focus on whatever may have been left unsaid. What surprised me as I listened was that although (almost) everyone cared about the dogs

LEFT Too often love is left out of the conversation about pit bulls and breed-specific legislation.

and their future, few people thought to speak about the thing that matters most. People quoted laws and statistics, but perhaps because it was a conference, no one spoke about the thing that can't be measured: love.

Our first night there I met Toni Phillips from Mariah's Promise, a rescue that had been taking in dogs expelled from Denver due to the law requiring that all pit bulls be put to death. Toni and her husband had come down to the conference with two of their dogs, and we played with them in the parking lot at the end of the day before they all headed out to find a hotel.

The next morning, they told me a terrifying story: they had checked into a national hotel chain that advertises itself as pet friendly. They had paid the deposit and headed to bed. Just as they and their two dogs were drifting off to sleep together, there was a knock on the door. Someone had spotted the dogs and called the police, and the police were there to tell them they had to leave immediately.

Later that morning, I spoke to everyone about my own dogs. Many of the people in the room had volunteered after Katrina. I told the story of leaving with my dogs, and how Sula panicked and ran off that morning, but I was able to catch up with her and we were safe. We were some of the lucky ones. Everyone in the room understood the tragedy of dogs that were separated from their owners during Katrina. "That's what breed-specific legislation does," I said. "It separates families from their pets. And that is all it accomplishes."

The earliest laws regarding breed-specific legislation in the United States date back to July 1987—the same month that *Sports Illustrated* warned everyone to "BEWARE OF THIS DOG." Yet, in that time, there has been no evidence that breed-specific laws have accomplished anything, which is why so many areas that have had the laws in place are now in the process of overturning them. But those of us who love our dogs—dogs of any breed—need to continue being vigilant in demonstrating the best of what they bring to our communities. Our mission, on behalf of our dogs, is to celebrate them in every way we can. We can celebrate them through training and through making sure they are a valued part of our families. We can celebrate them through choosing to spay and neuter in order to reduce the enormous numbers of them that are euthanized each year in public animal shelters.

One thing that makes pit bulls a fascinating subject is the extreme reactions they provoke in people's imaginations and thoughts. These impressions of the breed often reflect the inner workings of their own minds rather than anything to do with the dogs themselves. Their reactions are based on accepted generalities rather than rational, individual evaluation and thought. Gandhi said that the character of a nation can be judged by how it treats its animals, and the history of the American pit bull says both the best and the worst about us.

But while other people may look at our dogs and see mythical beasts, we can remind ourselves that we are lucky—because we really see them, their beauty and intelligence, and the value they bring to our lives.

RIGHT While two pit bulls stand watch, a third gives her mom, Ami Ciontos, a kiss.

ACKNOWLEDGMENTS

Several years ago, after the success of *The Dogs Who Found Me*, I proposed doing a book that might have been similar to this one. Might have been, but wasn't, because none of the publishers I met with felt comfortable handling such a controversial topic. Or they wanted to tread lightly, cheaply, and with minimal support. Eventually, I put the idea aside and moved on to other things.

Then a funny thing happened. Editor Kristin Mehus-Roe e-mailed me to ask if I might consider writing a book celebrating the American pit bull. Easy question to answer! This book would not exist if not for her unwavering faith and dedication. Nor would it be possible without the support of everyone at becker&mayer! and Viking Studio. My guide on the Viking Studio side of things is the wonderful Megan Newman, who introduced herself with a photo of the Rottweiler she found on the way to work.

Thanks, too, go out to the dogs and the people who agreed to participate in the book, as well as Animal Farm Foundation, BAD RAP, and the Helen Keller archive at the American Foundation for the Blind.

And last but not least, I'd like to thank the following for allowing me to take the time to finish this book: everyone at the Sula Foundation, Maple Street Book Shop, NOCCA, and Canine Connection. Most patient of all: my wonderful dogs, Brando, Zephyr, Douglas, and Bananas; and my permanent foster dog, Dominick.

BIOGRAPHY

Ken Foster is the author of the best seller *The Dogs Who Found Me* and its sequel, *Dogs I Have Met*, as well as a collection of short stories, *The Kind I'm Likely to Get*. His work has been featured in *Time Out New York*, the *New York Times Book Review*, *Bark*, and other publications. He lives in New Orleans with his dogs Brando, Zephyr, Douglas, and Bananas, where he is the founder of the Sula Foundation.

RESOURCES

The following is a selection of resources for pit bull owners and anyone who wishes to learn more about the dogs. As you may already know or expect, even among pit bull lovers there are differences of opinion on what is best for our dogs. This sampling of resources is a great place to start and should lead, inevitably, to additional sources of pit bull ed:

Education, Advocacy, and Rescue
Animal Farm Foundation: www.animalfarmfoundation.org
BAD RAP: www.badrap.org
Best Friends Animal Society: www.bestfriends.org
Game Dog Guardian: www.gamedogguardian.com
National Canine Research Council: http://nationalcanineresearchcouncil.com/publications/suggested-reading/
Our Pack, Inc: www.ourpack.org
The Sula Foundation: www.sulafoundation.org
StubbyDog: www.stubbydog.org

Training and Enrichment
Association of Pet Dog Trainers: www.apdt.com
Dog Star Daily: www.dogstardaily.com
Sirius Dog Training: www.siriuspup.com
Patricia McConnell: www.patriciamcconnell.com
Clicker Training: www.clickertraining.com
Dogs and Storks: www.dogsandstorks.com
Quick and Easy Crate Training by Teoti Anderson
Before and After You Get Your Puppy by Ian Dunbar
How to Teach an Old Dog New Tricks by Ian Dunbar
Ruff Love by Susan Garrett
Play Together Stay Together by Patricia McConnell
Don't Shoot the Dog by Karen Pryor
Living with Kids and Dogs by Colleen Pelar
How to Behave So Your Dog Behaves by Sophia Yin
Culture Clash by Jean Donaldson
Inside of a Dog by Alexandra Horowitz
Really Reliable Recall by Leslie Nelson
Dog Training for Children by Ian Dunbar

Additional Reading
American Pitbull by Marc Joseph
Bandit: Dossier of a Dangerous Dog by Vicki Hearne
The Dogs Who Found Me by Ken Foster
The Lost Dogs: Michael Vick's Dogs and Their Tale of Rescue and Redemption by Jim Gorant: www.thelostdogsbook.com
The Pit Bull Placebo: The Media, Myths, and Politics of Canine Aggression by Karen Delise:

http://nationalcanineresearchcouncil.com/publications/ncrc-publications/
Pit Bulls & Pit Bull Type Dogs: 82 Dogs the Media Doesn't Want You to Meet by Melissa McDaniel: http://photobooks.myshopify.com/collections/frontpage/products/pit-bull-photo-book-pre-order
"Troublemakers: What Pit Bulls Can Teach Us about Profiling" by Malcolm Gladwell (*The New Yorker*, February 6, 2006 www.newyorker.com/archive/2006/02/06/060206fa_fact); also appears in his book *What the Dog Saw.*

BIBLIOGRAPHY
Applebome, Peter. "A Pit Bull Who Provided Lessons in Loyalty and Unfailing Love." *The New York Times*, March 28, 2007, B1.

Bradley, Janis. "The Relevance of Breed in Selection of Companion Dogs." National Canine Research Council, 2011.

Cooper, Jackie. *Please Don't Shoot My Dog.* New York: William Morrow & Co., 1981.

Duncan, Dayton. *Horatio's Drive: America's First Road Trip.* New York: Knopf, 2003.

Gladwell, Malcolm. "Troublemakers." *The New Yorker*, February 6, 2006.

Gorant, Jim. *The Lost Dogs*. New York: Gotham Books, 2010.

Gorant, Jim. "What Happened to Michael Vick's Dogs . . ." *Sports Illustrated*, December 2008.

Hearne, Vicki. *Bandit: Dossier of a Dangerous Dog*. New York: Harper Collins, 1991. Reissued as *Bandit: The Heart-warming True Story of One Dog's Rescue from Death Row* by Skyhorse Publishing, 2007.

Hendrix, Steve. "Racked by PTSD, a veteran finds calm in a pound pup named Cheyenne." *The Washington Post*, June 21, 2011.

Humes, Immy, director. *A Little Vicious*. The Doc Tank, Inc., 1991.

Joseph, Marc. *American Pitbull*. Göttingen: Steidl, 2005.

Keller, Helen. *The Story of My Life*. Garden City, NY: Doubleday, 1903.

Kudlinski, Kathleen and Henderson, Meryl. *Dr. Seuss: Young Author and Artist*. New York: Aladdin, 2005.

Lee, Shayne. "Punishing Vick for Our Crimes." *The Philadelphia Inquirer*, May 26, 2009.

Morgan, Judith and Morgan, Neil. *Dr. Seuss & Mr. Geisel: A Biography*. New York: Random House, 1995.

Staub, Andrew. "Abused Pottsville Pit Bull Lands Role in 'Oliver!'" *Pottsville Republican-Herald*, July 17, 2007, T2.

Swift, E.M. "The Pit Bull: Friend and Killer." *Sports Illustrated*. July 27, 1987.

Thurber, James. *Thurber: Writings and Drawings*. New York: Library of America, 1996.

The Little Rascals: The Complete Collection (DVD). Genius Entertainment, 2008.

PHOTOGRAPHER BIOGRAPHY

Karen Morgan is a Chicago-based nationally recognized commercial photographer with an emphasis in people and animal portraiture. Her immense passion for animals, especially the relationship between humans and dogs, is a focus in both her personal and commercial work. Morgan owns two rescued pit bulls, and created the "Not My Pitbull" photographic project (www.notmypitbull.com).
www.kmorganphoto.com

IMAGE CREDITS

Cover, contents page, back cover, pages 8, 14, 18, 21, 22, 23 (both), 24, 34, 37, 39, 40-41, 42, 44-45, 47, 48, 52, 68, 70-71, 72, 77, 86, 98, 103, 106, 122, 130, 132-133, 134, 136, and 144: © Karen Morgan Photography

Pages 16-17, 28, 56, 57, 110, 111, 113, and 125: Courtesy of Animal Farm Foundation

Page 11: Courtesy of Ken Foster

Page 12: © Kathy Anderson/Times-Picayune

Page 15: Courtesy of The Sula Foundation

Page 27: Courtesy of Anita Joe

Page 31: © 1990 Enrico Ferorelli

Page 33: Courtesy Sandy Chism

Page 35: © Melissa Lipani

Page 36: © AP Photo/Michael Poche

Page 46: Courtesy of Gary Lassere

Page 51: Courtesy of Theo Cooper

Page 54: Courtesy of Jennifer Shryock

Page 58: Courtesy of Kelly Shutt Cottrell

Page 60: © St. Louis Post-Dispatch

Page 62: Collection of Margaretha Owens and Ted Owens

Page 63: Courtesy of Aneta Lagos

Page 65: Courtesy of Ledy VanKavage

Page 66: Courtesy of Lynn Terry

Page 69: © Kara Stokes Photography

Page 74: © Melissa Lipani

Page 76: © Paw Prints Charming Pet Photography, courtesy of Hillary Kladke

Page 78: © AP Photo/Nick Ut

Page 80: Courtesy of Donna Reynolds/BAD RAP

Page 82: Courtesy of Jessica Funderburk

Page 83: Courtesy of Kristen Horn

Page 84: © AP Photo/The Columbian, Steven Lane

Page 87: © AP Photo/Eric Risberg

Page 89: Courtesy of Dan Hagen

Page 91: Courtesy of Letti de Little

Page 92: © Simon Bruty/Sports Illustrated/Getty Images

Page 93: Public domain image courtesy of Robert Saltzman

Page 94-95: Courtesy of Jordyn Goldbach

Page 96: © Melissa Lipani

Page 101: © Diana Pappas

Page 102: Courtesy of Donna Reynolds/BAD RAP

Page 104: © Library of Congress/digital version by Science Faction/Getty Images

Page 108: New York Daily Tribune, July 30, 1903/ Library of Congress

Page 109: Courtesy of Marthina McClay

Page 112: Courtesy National Geographic, Crown Copyright, British Press Services

Page 115: © Joshua Grenell

Page 117: © Timothy White, courtesy of Bernadette Peters

Page 118: © AP Photo/Jae C. Hong

Page 120: Courtesy of Tim Racer

Page 121: Courtesy of Donna Reynolds

Page 127: © Mike Bailey Photography

Page 128: © Todd Cerveris

Page 131: © J. Avery Wham

Page 138-139: Courtesy of Ami Ciontos

Design elements (throughout): Scuffed brown leather texture © Duncan Walker/iStockphoto; Grungy Brushed Brass Sign © AlexMax/iStockphoto.

143

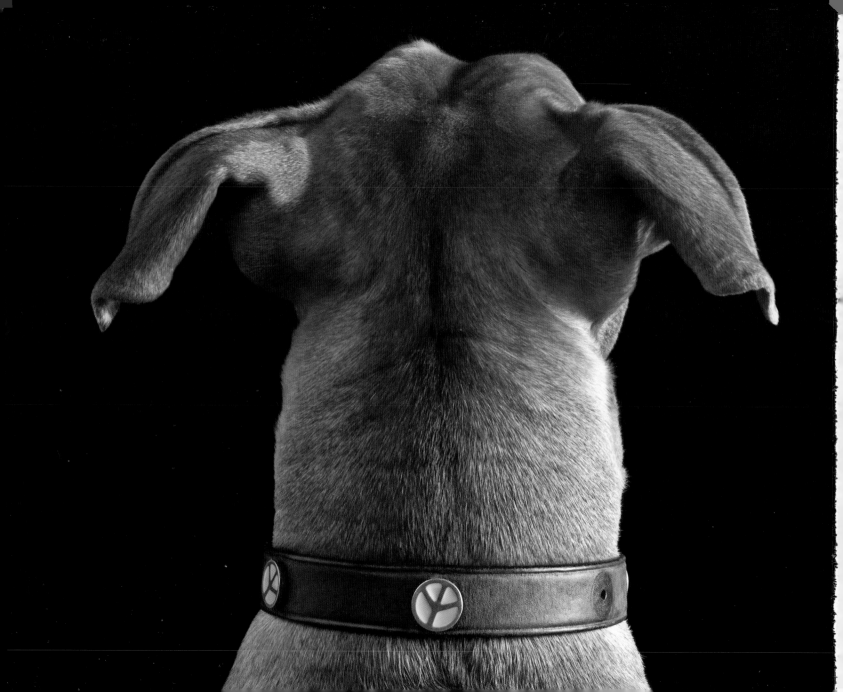